Living the Mass

Living
the Mass

*The Ordinary of the Mass and . . .The
Ordinary of Life*

By F. DESPLANQUES, S.J.

translated by SISTER MARIA CONSTANCE
Sister of Charity of Halifax

THE NEWMAN PRESS • Westminster, Maryland
1953

First published March, 1951
Second printing July, 1951
Third printing November, 1951
Fourth printing February, 1952
Fifth printing September, 1952
Sixth printing January, 1953
Seventh printing October, 1953

Contents

Foreword

Back in 1910, Gilbert K. Chesterton wrote *What's Wrong with the World?* His biographer, Maisie Ward, tells us that Gilbert was still asking that question while writing his book. In 1940, Father Desplanques, S.J., answered it. The Chestertonian accent in his answer comes from the fact that not once while writing his book did the learned Jesuit ask himself the question. Nevertheless, as you close his work after the first, second, or fifth reading—yes, it is that kind of a book! you go back to it again and again!—the conviction that he has shown us just what is wrong with the world stands out in your mind clearer than letters of flame ever stood out on a wall of black velvet. *We* are the answer! Especially we Christians: most especially we Catholics. We have been—and yet are—on the road to Damascus, the road to Emmaus, and the road to Jericho. Small wonder, then, that the world is on the road to disintegration.

But do understand me: there is nothing wrong with any of the roads we are on provided we are knocked from our horse and blinded outside Damascus, have our eyes opened at Emmaus, and allow a Samaritan to pick us up half-dead by the Jericho roadside. Father Desplanques' book does all three things.

Now while it is true that we Christians, and especially we Catholics, have not been riding toward Damascus "breathing out threats of slaughter," it is, alas! too true that we have been as ignorant as was Saul of that world-revolutionizing, because self-dignifying and "self"-destroying, doctrine that Christians and Christ are one. We have not been walking to Emmaus with hearts heavy because of hopes dead; but, surely, somehow or other, "our eyes have been held," so that we have not recognized the Stranger who joins us on the way—not even "in the breaking of the Bread!" That we have "fallen among robbers" on our way to Jericho, that Materialism, Secularism, and modern Skepticism have left us "half-dead," is all too obvious even to the least observant.

But the Good Samaritan is at hand, not with oil and wine, but with something infinitely better—*Bread and Wine!* Out of that twenty-centuries-old Revelation of Revelations, Father Desplanques has made a new revelation by showing us that we have not remembered those few things we should never forget. One such is that "the Mass is the supreme expression of the Love of God." Another is that the Son said of His Father: *"Pater mea agricola est*—My Father is the husbandman."—"Alas, O God!" exclaims the Jesuit author, "Thy children, little and great, forget it. To an ever greater extent we find people who have never known it. School books no longer teach it. Since the beginning of the twentieth century some even pretend that Thy wheat grows by itself and that the mills turn better without Thee. Result:—the barns are bursting, the granaries are cracking under the sacks—and the poorest of Thy children go without bread." Perhaps our greatest sin of forgetfulness lies in the fact that we have not remembered that the midmost moment of all time was the ninth hour on the 14th day of the month of Nisan—and that that moment is eternal! Father Desplanques makes that moment as intimate and as personal as it really was and is by saying: "Yesterday, on the 14th day of the month of Nisan, at the ninth hour—we say at three o'clock in the afternoon—Thou sawest me just as I am now, occupied in writing . . . or in weeding my garden . . . or in sewing . . . or in laboring . . . or in suffering, perhaps. And Thou didst love me with an ineffable love. . . . To me Thou didst dedicate Thy last sigh, the last drop of Thy Blood . . . in one great cry." Oh, if we had only remembered that! If we will only remember it now, how different the world will be!

So as not to mislead, let me say that Father Desplanques gave no thought whatsoever to what was wrong with the world. His one concern was with how to set the world right. With a wisdom that is more than human he shows us how to do that by giving us as the solution for our every problem exactly what the Omniscient God gave us. Father Desplanques gives us—*Christ!*

To many a Christian that will not sound like a new solution; to the non-Christian it will not sound like a solution at all; yet, it is the only solution that is sound. Father Desplanques does not say what has so often been said, namely, that the world needs Christianity. What he says is that the world needs CHRIST! Sad to say, there is a difference between the two. It is the Christianity of old that can save us, and only that. Which means that we modern Christians must walk not "in the fiery footprints left on the earth by the saints," but in the blood-red footprints left on the road that leads to Calvary by the Saint of saints. In short, what Father Desplanques has said is that we must *make the Mass our life, and our life a Mass.*

That is the meaning of the subtitle to his work: "The Ordinary of the Mass and . . . The Ordinary of Life." The author was most careful in his choice of words; for throughout his work his insistence is on what is most ordinary in the ordinary life of the ordinary man, and he shows how all this fits into the Ordinary of the Mass, and how the Ordinary of the Mass fits into it. There, precisely, is the new "revelation" he makes out of the age-old Revelation of Revelations. Do not think me extravagant. I am only being exact. His work is not a translation; it is not an interpretation; it is not an exegesis nor an elaboration. It is really a revelation of our sublime dignity, our duty, and our divine destiny; a revelation of all we are, and all we have, and all we can, all we must do for God, ourselves, and our neighbor as we go our ordinary way in the ordinary circumstances of our lives. It is also a revelation of how deaf, dumb, and blind we have been all our ordinary lives—especially how dumb!

As we search the "unsearchable ways of God," it seems most patent that His Providence has reserved a rediscovery of the Doctrine of the Mystical Body of Christ for our day of dictators and destruction. Abbé Anger was among the first to show that this truth is the white heart of the Kohinoor which is Catholic dogma, but it awaited Father Desplanques to show us the heart of that heart. He bares the center's central core when he "reveals" the truth not only that Catholic laymen are priests, but that the life of the ordinary Catholic layman can be, should be, must be the life of the one great and only Catholic Highpriest. He does this when he shows that, like Christ, the Christian has only one thing to do—to offer the Sacrifice of the Mass!

"I have a Baptism wherewith I am to be baptised," said Christ, "and how am I straitened until it be accomplished" (Lc. 12, 50). We know it was a Baptism of Blood. We know it was a Death, a Resurrection, and an Ascension. What we have not known, and what Father Desplanques teaches us, is that we have the same baptism wherewith we must be baptised, and that we will live in straits unless we accomplish it. The tragedy of this tragedy is that we have all the elements at hand, yet do not inform them; we have the body, but do not inject the soul. His Passion—our "passion"—is being renewed again and again, but mankind is not being regenerated simply because we are not "Mass-conscious," "Christ-conscious," "God-conscious," divinely "self-conscious" men. We have not realized that we and Christ are one. Hence we know little of our worth as persons, our wealth as Christians, or the weight of our obligations as members of Christ.

How we need to pray to God with the author for "this ardent conviction: that not a hair falls from our heads without Thy permission; that in Thy hands emperors and dictators are as pawns, even as am I, or any poor fool . . . and that behind the curtain of appearances week by week, day by day, minute by minute Thou controllest the whole scenario of the centuries and the years . . . Yes, despite all that, for the Grand Drama of Love, Thou claimest from Thy child his two arms, his two feet, his whole soul, his whole heart even to its last pulsation."

That is how Father Desplanques thinks, how he writes, how he prays. Yes, he prays. For this is not only a book; it is a prayer-book and a pocket-book! The wealth it holds is overwhelming. In his introduction he has begged us not to *read* his book. His plea is utterly unnecessary; for what he has written cannot be read. It can only be pondered in wonder, awe, and love—reflected upon with deep, deep sorrow and ever mounting joy. For its every thought stops and stimulates, gives both pause and impulse, generates thought and inspires HOPE.

What the genesis of his book was, he does not say. In his preface he cites *Miserentissimus Redemptor*, the Encyclical of Pius XI in which the priesthood of the laity is stressed. In the same preface he makes mention of Catholic Action; and, thank God, we are coming to realize that *the* Catholic Action is the Mass! But perhaps Father has indicated the real source of the work when he so pithily and penetratingly says: "We have mediocre Christians because their Mass is mediocre." Never was a truth more truthfully told, nor a condition more accurately traced to its cause. We Christians are in great part the real causes of our world's sad condition; and the sad cause of our condition is our ignorance of the interrelation and the interpenetration of "the ordinary of our life and the Ordinary of the Mass."

The genesis of this translation, however, can be told in one word—*love*. Sister Maria Constance knew she had found treasure when she found *La Messe*. During a period of convalescence, after a very serious surgical operation, her Christ-heart went out to her friend in Christ, Sister Mary Clare. With her she must share the treasure. But as superioress of a very large convent and principal of a much larger school, Sister Mary Clare would have little leisure to translate the French. Sister Maria Constance would use the leisure of her convalescence for this work of double love—love for Christ and love for her friend in Christ. Sister Mary Clare had hardly read the first few pages when she thought of one who little merits the lavish sisterly love she has ever shown him. I had not passed beyond page three of the Introduction before I was saying: "This must be published! How our Catholics need to know that 'the priest at the altar has need of THEIR fervor'; that

'CHRIST is expecting something from THEM'; that
'Souls whom they love are DEPENDING on them'; that
'Everywhere, silently, they are beseeching: "Come! *Collaborate!*" '

How our Catholics need to know that Christ, 'the Divine Poor Man,' is crying:

'Give Me what is still wanting to My Passion!
'Give Me the painful labor of YOUR hands! the suffering of YOUR heart! YOUR tears! YOUR flesh and blood! Give Me YOUR life!' "

How often we have heard a cry for the Mass "in the vernacular," so that the people could understand "what was going on." Well, here it is! But instead of helping to understand "what is going on," it makes us alarmingly conscious of the fact that we must "carry on" for Christ, with Christ, and in Christ. How often have we heard discussions of the necessity for, and of the ways and means of, bringing our "Sunday religion" into our work-day, week-day life. Well, here is how! As the author points out, a priest cannot go into a workshop, a machine-shop, or a factory in chasuble and alb. Not even in his cassock. But you, you laymen, you priests by Baptism and Confirmation, you other-Christs, "without any other ornament than your working-clothes, can offer up to God, through the Christ of the Mass, all the work, all that activity, all that human labor which must not be lost. Christ, in you, will transform it into adoration and love."

I know there will be some who will say that this book is not for the ordinary run of the people. These are the ones who would have said the same thing about St. Paul's Epistles to the Corinthians, the Ephesians, the Galatians, and the Colossians at the very time Paul wrote them. These are the ones who are wiser than the all-wise Holy Ghost under whose direction—I had almost said "dictation"—Paul wrote. Thank God that the more wise Catholics are now admitting that God did not reveal the Doctrine of the Mystical Body bootlessly; that it is a truth, a revelation, and most pertinent to our times. Whenever this question arises, I like to ask what Emile Mersch, S.J., asked in the Introduction to his monumental work *The Whole Christ*—"Is it to be regretted that God should have given us a union with His Son that transcends our own limited views? . . . Are there truths in our religion that are dangerous? truths that must be avoided? truths that, by their very nature, are capable of engendering only false notions and vain discussions?" But what I like better is to point out to our enlightened age the I.Q. of the audience to which God the Holy Ghost addressed this doctrine. The Church of Corinth was not an aristocracy of intellectuals! It was made up, as Christ's Church has ever been, and shall ever be, of people from all ranks and all classes; but the bulk was, as the bulk is and ever will be, not from the schools, but from the stores, the docks, the shops, and the streets! They understood the doctrine! Can't we?

Father Desplanques thinks so; for time and again he addresses "the sweeper with her broom, the seamstress with her needle and scissors, the stenographer with her notebook and pencil, the housekeeper with her market-bag . . . this rich man, this laborer, this servant, this society lady . . . those with a brush in their hand, or a shovel, a pickaxe, or a fountain pen, a broom, a pair of scissors or a fork. . . ." Just exactly the audience the Holy Ghost addressed through Paul! This Jesuit priest has seen what that intrepid Apostle saw, namely, that the life of a merchant, manufacturer, lawyer, banker, artisan, or simple laborer is not life unless he becomes a Christ-merchant, a Christ-manufacturer, a Christ-lawyer, a Christ-banker, a Christ-artisan, or a Christ-laborer. He sees that the whole purpose of life is that, if we cannot reduce to zero the number of the damned, we can, at least, each day, increase the number of the blessed. He sees that man was made to serve God our Father, to serve our brothers and sisters in Christ, and not to serve ourselves. He sees with a rare clarity that "the Cross is the axis of the world and that this planet is the Repository for the Host." Pascal never thought deeper thoughts nor did Claudel express them more beautifully.

But the point at issue is the practicality of such thoughts and expression. If anyone will think a moment on the revolutions this Doctrine has effected since the time Christ first spoke of the "vine and branches" and Paul wrote of the "Head and members"; if one will see the society of the ancient world slowly changed from a society in which, literally, the slaves were countless, into the medieval society, in which slaves had become serfs, and serfs were rapidly becoming freedmen—and all because "we are one in Christ"; if one will think of the numberless captives made during those ages when war and insecurity filled prisons much as our modern dictators have filled concentration camps, and then think of the religious orders, such as the Mercedarians and the Trinitarians, established just to ransom these captives—and all because Christ said: "I was in prison and you visited Me"; if one will think of how the poor in Apostolic times were cared for by the rich of Jerusalem; in the Roman Empire, right down to the time of the Protestant Revolt, by the Church; in the Middle Ages by those who erected and conducted orphanages, homes for the aged, and the guest-houses in every monastery; if one will remember that the Papal

States were called "the patrimony of the poor" just because the revenues from them went to the poor; if one will awake to the fact that from the fourth to the sixteenth century not a sermon on charity nor an appeal for funds was ineffective—simply because they were based on the truth that "whatsoever you do to these . . . you do to Me!"—then one might cease to question the practicality of the most practical doctrine ever given to man. If we are to believe the words Christ spoke, we get to Heaven or we go to Hell precisely because we have lived, or failed to live this doctrine which says Christians and Christ are one!

In our day practicality is recognized only when it shows social, political, or economic results. That is why I like to call attention to the fact that "hospitals" were unknown in pre-Christian times; that the first "modern hospital"—truly a medical center!—was erected by St. Basil of Caesarea in 369; that the great medieval Orders of Knighthood, such as the Knights of St. John, the Knights Templars, and the Teutonic Knights, worked in hospitals—and that the motive of it all was: "I was sick and you visited Me!" In our day we have seen much, a great deal too much, of racism and nationalism; what enough of us haven't seen is that the Catholic Church has always opposed racism, that St. Peter condemned it in the First Council of Jerusalem, that St. Paul was tireless in his insistence on the fact that "there is neither Jew, barbarian, or Scythian, for Christ is all in all" (Col. 3, 11). And that is the Doctrine of the Mystical Body.

The Church did not stop, because she could not stop, the fall of the Roman Empire. The dry rot had set in before the Empire was Christianized. But what she could do, and what she did do, was to prevent Europe from lapsing into barbarism after the Empire's fall. She did it by uniting all human tribes in her bosom, breaking down the barriers of race, language, custom, and law, and teaching them to love one another since they were all members of the one body!

The same work is before the Church today. So are the

same means! It is worth while noting that the Holy Roman Empire was based on the Doctrine of the Mystical Body of Christ, and that Democracy rests on hardly any other foundation. Surely no one is going to insist that all men are created exactly equal in the face of the fact that no two men are ever born physically, intellectually, socially, or economically equal! Our equality comes from the fact that we are persons, and persons who can be incorporated in the Holy Trinity's Second Person. It is on that base we can hope to erect a sound and effective supranational institution which is to safeguard the liberties of the world—and on no other! For just as, in the final analysis, it is seen that our present-day chaos is the result of the denial of this doctrine, so it will be seen, by those who see ultimates, that the one remedy for our situation and the hope of the future lies in a reaffirmation of this doctrine; but an affirmation not in words, not in songs and slogans, not in placards and parades, but in the ordinary of our lives translated into the Ordinary of the Mass, and the Ordinary of the Mass made the core of our ordinary lives!

Since work and wages make up the ordinary of most of our lives, let it be said that even in the economic field this truth is fundamental. In his *Quadragesimo Anno* Pius XI said: "Then only will it be possible to unite all in harmonious striving for the common good, when all sections of society have the intimate conviction that they are members of a single family, children of the same heavenly Father, and further, that they are one body in Christ and everyone members one of another."

Now Father Desplanques has none of this in his book, and yet he has it all. What I mean is that you will read nothing of the above in his lines; yet you can read nothing else between his lines. He busied himself with the Mass only, but he showed us that our only business is the Mass.

A reflective reading of his work leads inevitably to the conclusion he expressed somewhere, namely, that "nothing but God is of importance any longer in my life." He has brought God near, made Him more intimate than your father, mother, or best friend, more important than your breath or heart-beat. "Teach me to pray!" has been the cry of every soul created. Father Desplanques teaches us as Christ taught us. He shows that we are syllables of the Word, particles of the Host, the drop of water in the wine to be consecrated. Having shown us that, he has shown us how we can save mankind; for as he has put it: "the sanctification of a single soul is one of the major elements in the reconstruction of the world."

If this Foreword seems volcanic, blame the book; for to enter into the spirit of the work is to enter into the very presence of God with the consequent eruption of fear that Presence inspires and the ebullition of love that Presence inflames. The author has made time stop and given us a sense of that "perpetual present" which is Eternity; for he links the Mass now being offered by you and me and the entire Mystical Body of Christ, not only with the first Mass ever offered, that of the Cenacle, but with those said in the dark of the Catacombs on the still warm bodies of the latest martyrs, and with those magnificent Masses of the later centuries said by the Pope or a Bishop with twenty, thirty, fifty, or a hundred co-consecrating priests, yes, and with the last Mass to be said perhaps some ten hundred or ten thousand years from now just before the trump of doom. It makes one think that the Greeks in demanding the triple unity of time, place, and persons were foreshadowing the triple unity of the world's greatest Drama, wherein time was caught up by the Timeless, the universe by its Creator, and all persons in the Godhead's Second Person.

Someone has said: "It is the Mass that matters!" After going through Father Desplanques' book, one cannot escape the conclusion that nothing else does matter.

FR. M. RAYMOND, O.C.S.O.

Oct. 13, 1949.

Preface

In the very august Eucharistic Sacrifice, the priests and the rest of the faithful must join their immolation in such a way that they offer themselves also as living hosts, holy and agreeable to God.

Elect race, royal priesthood (I Peter II, 9), they must concur in this oblation almost in the same manner as the priest.

(PIUS XI: *Miserentissimus Redemptor.*)

What great clarity there is in this text of Pius XI, which we set here in relief, concerning the rôle of a simple Christian in the Mass!

The expression "priesthood of the faithful," it is true, does not appear here, but the text of Saint Peter applied to the laity, *genus electum . . . regale sacerdotium*, suggests it clearly; and when the Pope says that the "faithful must concur in this oblation in almost the same manner as the priest," what does he say if not that, apart from the Consecration and the mediation between the people and God—which belong personally and exclusively to the celebrant—the rest of the Sacrifice concerns the whole Church.

The Church, then, even in the person of those who are merely baptised, has a part to play, in which it is irreplaceable. The faithful must participate in the Mass, *Offering the Host with the Priest and* OFFERING THEMSELVES WITH THE HOST. *There* is the source of their grandeur and their holiness.

Our young people, so active in the various forms of Catholic Action, and stirred into new vigor by their spiritual directors, have understood this so well! Would that the generality of Christians would follow their lead!

The fusion of souls in the *"cor unum et anima una"* of the Prayer of Christ still leaves much to be desired. And yet it is a matter of traditional doctrine which has been lived and practiced through centuries by ordinary Christian people. We should like to restore to souls the knowledge of a Mass which is truly an immolation as well as the "Sacrament of Unity."

It is not to be wondered at that we have mediocre Christians, if their Mass is mediocre. At a time when, more and more, the laity is being asked to collaborate with the hierarchy, the first form of collaboration which presents itself between priest and faithful is that of the Holy Sacrifice.

Catholic Action depends upon the way in which those who direct it, priests and faithful, will say the Mass, will collaborate and sacrifice themselves with Christ crucified. To whoever would understand it better, the following pages offer, in a very simple and practical way, a little material for meditation and adoration.

Introduction to the Mystery

I

FOR APPRENTICESHIP
IN THE MOST BEAUTIFUL OF SERVICES

Servant of God, man or woman, old or young,
 apprenticed in the Sacrifice of Jesus Christ . . .
   above all things, do not read this book during Mass!
Indeed, do not *read* this book at all . . .
 before, during, nor after!
 Rather, MEDITATE it!
Pray with it! . . . in order that, slowly . . . gradually . . .
 (such a long time is needed for that) . . . you may learn:
 to participate in the Sacrifice,
 to unite with the priest during Mass,
 through the customary responses,
 through the DOUBLE OBLATION of Christ and you
 yourself.

   It would be a mistake for a seminarian . . .

to learn to celebrate . . .
 only in celebrating.
 You can see the folly of that!
Pre-occupied with himself and his actions . . .
 what would remain in him for Love!
If, on the contrary, he comes to the altar with a feeling of confidence that his body is prepared for the rites according to
 the rubrics . . .
 fearlessly, without need of support . . .
 he will cast himself, with all his soul, into the profound
 Mystery.

learn from the beginning to follow the priest carefully.
Form the habit . . .
> of finding the page in your missal quickly,
> of not losing five minutes, every time, looking for it,
> of putting the soul into the words.

Learn, also, to break the habit . . .

every day . . . of making the Sign of the Cross mechanically
> . . . of thoughtlessly stammering *Amen* and *Et cum Spiritu tuo,*
> of that practice which means paralysis of body, spirit, and heart.

At all cost, keep your fervor from growing cold . . . do not
> let the divine honey of the sacred words become insipid.
> Do all you can . . . so that each time your Offertory may be more sincere;
> so that each time your immolation may be more real.

Worst of all . . . is to let yourself become *accustomed* to the Mass.

"But . . . I am not a priest! . . ."

I understand . . .
You are not really a priest.
> But you are baptised and confirmed, and that is wonderful in itself!
> For that is enough to qualify you to collaborate.
> "The faithful," said Pius XI, "must concur in this oblation in almost the same manner as the priest . . ." (*Miserentissimus Redemptor*)
> and Saint Cyprian: "If our oblation and our sacrifice do not correspond with the Passion of Christ, the Sacrifice of the Lord is not celebrated with the required holiness." (*id.*)

The priest at the altar, then, has need of your fervor.

4

Christ is expecting something from you.
Souls whom you love are depending on you.
    Everywhere, silently, they beseech you,
    "Come! Collaborate! . . ."

                                Collaborate . . . that is to say,

Offer your whole self!
Offer the Body of your God with the priest, with the Church!
Fulfill your Service!
Do not lose an iota of your privilege!
    Take your full share in the priesthood . . .
    Whether you be Simon of Cyrene or Veronica,
    married or single, rich or poor,
    even a little boy or a little girl . . .
Christ and His priest are awaiting you and saying:
    "Help! Do not remain a useless spectator. Enter with us
    into the drama.
    Follow us wherever we go."

                                That supposes an apprenticeship

to put your soul into the right atmosphere . . .
That supposes that you have meditated, often, on each part of
    the Mass,
        so that at each response, at each word, at each stroke of the
        little bell, at the Kyrie, at the Gospel, at the Credo, at the
        Offertory, at the Consecration, at the Pater,
        and finally at the Communion,
you may be an ideal Veronica with her linen all ready,
you may be a Cyrenean with hands free,
you may be the servant or the handmaid at the most beautiful of
    services:
        ready to fill up what is wanting in the sufferings of Jesus
        Christ.
"My son, My daughter . . . My child," says this Divine Poor

Man, stretching out His hand,
"Have pity on Me!
Give Me what is still wanting in My Passion!
Give Me the PAINFUL LABOR of THY HANDS!
Give Me the SUFFERING of THY HEART!
Give Me THY TEARS!
Give Me thy flesh and thy blood!
GIVE ME THY LIFE! . . ."

To cooperate in the Mass, to live in it always,
   even when one has not received the Sacrament of Orders,
   is a great art!

But . . . in this age of Catholic Action,

now, when the Sovereign Pontiffs are urging the laity to be the
   extension of the priest, to go whither he cannot go,
what comfort for you . . . what a spur in this thought:
   In the innermost fibers of my being, I am marked with the
   figure of the Christ-Priest. I belong to Him, body and soul
   through my Baptism and my Confirmation, I am bound to
   His priesthood as to the priesthood of my pastor and of his
   curates and of all the priests of the Church. And just as
   together we offer the same Host in Sacrifice, *together*, each
   according to his state of life, we work for the conquest of
   souls. High or low, it is the same apostolic work, the great
   motivation of which is the Mass!
Pius XII, following the mind of Pius XI, declares in his first
   Encyclical:
   "This apostolic labor, accomplished according to the spirit
   of the Church, consecrates the layman, so to speak, and
   makes him a 'Minister of Christ.'"

What a difference there is . . .

in regarding the Mass and the redemption of souls as the ex-

6

clusive work of priests, under the pretext that one has no
part in it,
and in saying, "It is my concern also! . . .
I must perform my rôle in it because that Host there on the
altar is mine as It is that of the priest . . . I can then, nay, I
MUST make use of It . . ."
That realization should be for you a great discovery . . . the
great news of every day.

Please! Understand clearly!

For one same apostolic work,
one same living Source is needed: The MASS.
Christ and all His priestly members—ordained, confirmed, baptised—must needs be found at the same table.
None must be wanting in appetite.
For them, the Mass which gives them the Host is the grand
rendezvous.

The grand rendezvous . . .

of the family,
where they grow closer to each other in the charity of
Christ . . .
where they get new life . . .
where they regain an inspiration for the common task,
where they feel themselves truly servants and brothers,
where they learn the greatest Act of Love, which is to give
one's life for those one loves.
Daily, the great sacerdotal family of the Church must go up to
the table and eat together the Flesh of Christ, and drink His
Blood, in order, from their superfluity, to nourish the multitude of poor souls, ever increasing . . .
who are OUTSIDE THE FAMILY and . . .
who never have Bread and
who never have Wine.

7

MEDITATION FOR THE ALTAR BOY,
THE SACRISTAN, and
THE OLD LADY OF THE SIX O'CLOCK MASS

The poor village priest . . . so alone, alas . . . is glad when
you answer him, holy old lady of the six o'clock Mass.
Old lady, indeed! For the young people, nowadays, do not
rise in the morning.
There are parishes . . . how many!
where the priest is alone at the altar,
without any other partner to his *"Oremus"* and his *"Dominus vobiscum"* than the benches.
And yet, at Mass . . . except for a very rare indult,
it is forbidden for the priest to be alone!
What more effective proof do we need that Christians must
cooperate?
Vae soli! Woe to the priest without an altar boy!
He can no longer PRAY.
For the grand, for the *One Prayer,*
the whole Church must be present.
A simple little urchin may represent it.
"If you are not as these little ones," Christ said.

His Spouse is like "these little ones."

She diminishes herself to the small dimensions of this child.
She reduces herself to the point of entering entirely . . .
with her confessors, and her popes, and her martyrs . . .
into this little mite!
She puts up with his distractions . . .
She accepts . . . by force of necessity . . .
his twistings and turnings . . .
his silly childish pranks . . . and . . .

even if his service be a scuffle,
in which the grand words of the dialogue, by his garbling,
lose their form and sense,
in which the wine is rushed away by short cuts . . .
it matters not.
The Church is *there!*

Sadly we say it! . . .

At one time, all the people joined in the singing and in making
the responses.
The PRAYER was of one soul.
Christ, the bishop, or the pope celebrating, the priests, the
faithful, the angels, and the saints . . . were but one puls-
ing body.
Together, they offered Christ . . .
Together, they offered themselves with Him . . .
Then . . . time marched on.
The multiplication of low Masses
necessitated individual servers, and,
finally, these entirely replaced the former.
Harassed people rid themselves of their service . . .
They found it simpler to impersonate *le grand seigneur* and to
take on domestics . . .
a servant . . .
But no! . . .
There are neither Greeks, nor Romans, nor masters, nor slaves
in the service of Jesus Christ . . .
We are all children of the house, *Domestici Dei,*
we are all servers!

Even the tiniest of altar boys . . .

represents all Christendom,
those Christians present in the church, and those who are
not.

He speaks and loves for all his brothers and sisters in Christ, for all bishops under the Pope.
He is the great Church in miniature.
Of all Christians present . . . he is the foremost,
> the most representative . . . the nearest to Christ . . .
> because he is the most closely united with the priest,
> and the most closely uniting, since he is the connecting link between the priest and the faithful.

With the priest, a branch on the vine which is Christ,
> the foundation on Apostles and prophets . . .
> *Super aedificati . . . ipso summo angulari lapide Christo Jesu.* (Eph. II, 19-20)
> However small he may be, here is a great Christian, standing securely on the Rock of Peter.

Surely he should not act like a little monkey.

Could he not be made to understand?

This hare-brained youngster—in default of a biretta . . .
> could not his silly head be weighted down by these grave thoughts:
> "They are all depending on me! . . . I am representing the Church . . .
> This is a serious matter . . . and my reason for being here is
> TO OFFER WITH THE PRIEST, IN THE NAME OF THE CHURCH,
> *the Body and the Blood of Jesus Christ.*"

The sacristans, all those working around the church, and the devout assistants, would do well also to think about this . . .
> and inject into this Mass, which threatens to be cold and solitary . . .
> a little serene gravity . . .
> a spark of radiant and fraternal enthusiasm.

10

In very deed, they should be the leaders in generosity and in
love . . .
for all those people who have fallen away . . .
who are no longer there, in their places, on Sunday . . .
who are distracted . . . bored, waiting for the Mass to
come to an end . . .
Indeed, yes! *This* must come to an end!

•   And it will end only . . .

when the Mass, Sunday or daily,
has retrieved among the generality of Christians

its youth and beauty . . .

only when the greater number of Christians will know:
That there is *need of them* in the Holy Sacrifice:
that they have an indispensable rôle to play in it . . .
It will end only when catechists, preachers, and authors no
longer hesitate to tell every Christian the full nobility of
his Baptism . . .
and his marvelous prerogatives.
Then, the Mass will become again what it never should have
ceased to be:
The grand mustering of the whole Church,
of all the "Holy Priestly Race," around the Host . . .
singing and making the responses together,
*and offering themselves with their Christ to the Infinite
Majesty.*

GOING TO MASS

Meditation on the Street

It is 7 o'clock, 8 o'clock, 10 o'clock . . . Sunday . . . and I
am on my way to Mass.
On the street, others whom I pass are going hunting or
fishing.

Others, dressed in their Sunday best, are not going any-where.
I long, dear Lord, for them . . . for myself too . . .
to bear to Thee the love and the spirit Thou desirest.

Waylay these souls . . .

In the parable of the banquet, take the part of the servant.
Compel them to enter into my Sacrifice,
all these footsore from their rounds of pleasure, all these
Samaritans—men and women—buried in sin.
Impress them into your soul . . . *compelle intrare.*
And while we are going together to offer My Body and My
Blood . . .
be their proxy.

Be their proxy! . . .

True! I am responsible for souls.
And I am going to negotiate their salvation.
The eternal life or death of a whole multitude depends on
my vote today, that is to say, on my heart, on my offering,
on my immolation.
The *Amen* which I am going to say with the entire Church
is going to weigh in the balance of the Redemption of man-kind.
Soon, at the altar, through the hands of the priest, I am going to
take the Host and the Chalice of Salvation,
for France, for Germany, for Italy, for China and Japan . . .
for my own neighborhood, for the dance hall, for the
nearby theatre, for my own household.

For our salvation and that of the whole world.

For years, alas! . . . I did not know it.
I went to Mass for myself,
to avoid committing a sin . . .

12

or just to receive consolation . . . dessert . . . to receive the *small* host of the layman,

persuaded that the *large* Host was not for me.

Other people gave me little concern . . .

present or absent . . . Japanese or German. I gave no thought even to those close to me.

I *assisted* at the Holy Sacrifice . . . in the pews . . . among those to whom the priest's back is turned, among those who give a dime to the usher for a seat.

I *assisted* . . . as one assists at a play, a moving picture, without having the right to say anything (at least, so I thought), to *do* anything.

But now that I am learning . . .

O marvelous fact! . . .

that "all the children of the Church are priests, that at Baptism they receive the unction which makes them participate in the priesthood. The host which they must offer to God is wholly spiritual, it is themselves" (St. Ambrose *In Lucam* V, 33);

that "all Christians are priests because they are members of the one Priest, Jesus Christ" (St. Augustine, *City of God*, D. XX, 10);

that "by our Baptism, the royal and sacerdotal dignity is communicated to us all. Rejoice in this elevation as an honor which you share with all the body of the Church" (St. Leo, S. 4, P.L.T. 54 c. 148–149);

that "the entire Christian people, 'chosen race, royal priesthood,' should participate in the burdens of the mystical Priesthood, in the satisfaction and Sacrifice . . . in almost the same manner as priests" (Pius XI, *Miserentissimus Redemptor*) . . .

Oh, dear Lord, how happy I am . . .

I, then, have this glory and this nobility, I, a humble Christian,

whoever I may be . . . laborer or executive, business man
great or small, little cabin boy or water boy . . . and this
little nursery maid, too, ahead of me . . . there . . . on
the sidewalk . . . and that little chap, the altar boy . . .
who is afraid of being late and is galloping along,
and that old lady in her shawl, with her Sacred Heart
badge . . .
and that venerable gentleman with his umbrella and his
red-edged prayer book . . .
we all have the honor and glory of having been raised from our
dust to this "holy race," to this "royal priesthood," of
which Saint Peter speaks in his Epistle, and of being able
thus . . . it is he again who speaks . . . "to offer sacrifice."
Oh, dear Lord, what joy! . . .

      I can *offer* the Holy Sacrifice of the Mass

and not only *assist* thereat.
It is not enough to *assist* when one can offer.
It is not enough to be a pillar, a candlestick, a statue, when one
can be a participant, when one can be a vital actor in the
greatest drama the world will ever know.
O Christ, Thou dost tell me through Thy Doctors—I remember
now—that the character impressed on the soul of every
Christian, through Thy Baptism, is a first seal; it is an initial
participation in Thy royal priesthood.
And Thou makest Thy sacerdotal imprint on our souls
stronger, placing a second stamp, that of Thy Confirmation.
I belong thus doubly to the Christ-Priest. I am marked twice
with His seal in the deepest recesses of my being.
This seal is on every baptised soul, strengthened in every confirmed soul . . .

      A priest in embryo . . .

I know that this beginning reaches its fulfillment only in the Sacrament of Holy Orders and has its plenitude only in the Episcopacy.

I know full well that I can only *listen* to the wonderful words of the Consecration without pronouncing them with efficacy.

But all the rest of the Sacrifice is mine; it belongs to everyone. I concur in almost the same manner as the priest at the altar.

Together we pray, together we offer the Victim.

Together we supplicate the Father through the Son.

We offer ourselves *with* the Host. Everything is done in the plural.

It is the entire Church that goes up to the altar, that takes its Christ, through the hands of the ordained priest, and offers Him to His Father—and offers Herself with Him for the redemption of souls.

Hurrying toward the door . . .

For it is almost time. In fact, I see the altar boy lighting the candles . . .

I can say to myself, with joyous emotion, that in going to Mass, I am going not only to receive Christ, but to offer Him *and to offer myself with Him.*

I can say to myself, I *must* say to myself, that the Host which I shall receive claims in return the host which I bear.

I can say to myself, I *must* say to myself, that with the Christ-Priest, with the entire Church, and with the priest at the altar, representing the Church . . .

I am going to play a formidable, perhaps decisive part in this drama, for certain souls whom I love.

And instinctively . . .

I begin with the priest who is descending the steps of the altar, to make the Sign of the Cross, and to say the antiphon of this *Judica me* which I never used to dare recite, of this psalm of youth and of transport in total self-surrender.

Instinctively I gather up all the weariness, all the little crosses, the tiniest words, the most obscure acts of my day to weigh down the Host,

and I say with my whole heart, with all my brethren in Christ:

"Yes, Lord," with Thee . . . "I will go up to the altar of my God."

FIRST PART

Going to Meet Christ

Going to Meet Christ

From the Psalm "Judica me" to the Offertory

To orientate your soul:

At one time . . .

this was the Mass of the Catechumens, that is to say, the pagans seeking to become Christians . . . It was necessary to form them, to transform them through the reading of the Epistle and the Gospel and by the homily which followed . . . Souls, lying like fallow land, purified before being sowed through Baptism, little by little began to relish Christ . . . Christ to be offered . . . Christ to be received . . . to relish the true Sacrifice:

a Novitiate . . . an apprenticeship in the most beautiful of Services.

Now . . .

follow suit . . .

A long time has passed since you were baptised . . . but are you no longer a catechumen?

Can you, before Wisdom Itself, boast of your knowledge? Can you, before Infinite Purity, profess yourself sufficiently pure? Do you really know anything of the great Mystery of Faith?

You must penetrate it . . . and each time more deeply.

Do you not also need a novitiate . . . in compunction, in greatness of soul, and in purity?

Then, *make great account of these opening prayers.*

They will produce in you beautiful and rare virtues: humility, holy desire of purification, eagerness for the Word of God, need of hearing the "grand news," and . . . when the Mass reaches the *Gloria* and the *Credo* . . . the joy of glorifying the Holy Trinity with the angels and the saints, and pride in affirming your Faith.

But you will miss this if you habitually come late to Mass.

But, you say, is it not enough to be in time for the Offertory?

On Sunday, yes! . . . strictly to satisfy the precept. But, in doing so, although you escape mortal sin, you do not avoid venial sin.

Judge yourself, then, in your mediocrity!

What kind of collaborator is he who runs breathless to throw his burden into the Offertory?

When does he bear a burden?

When does he bear anything?

When is he not late and disqualified for the Offering?

More often he is there, with no offering, only through threat of punishment . . . that is all!

Oh, paltry religion, which consists in not doing this, in not doing that . . . under pain of . . .

Have you then nothing "to do" at the Holy Sacrifice? nothing to prepare?

You are well aware, now, that you play an important part in this drama for which you must be in your place on time, to give the responses that are expected from you, and to be ready to meet your obligation in the Offertory.

These wonderful prayers of purification and of detachment and of enthusiasm and of love, this Law of Christ, told and retold in the Gospel and the Epistle, "that each one must bear his cross," will render you able, with hands full of what you have stripped from yourself to weigh down the Host.

20

Already Christ is announcing Himself. The Church claims your participation from the very first minute.

Who is the "foolish virgin" or the "wicked servant" if not he who, when Christ suddenly appears, finds himself before Him with hands empty?

Who is the "wise virgin" or the "courageous servant" if not he who nourishes and supports Christ in the poor . . . and why not? . . . in the Host?

Prepare! Go to Christ with hands full.

I

INTROIBO AD ALTARE DEI

I will go in unto the altar of God.

These are the first steps of the day's journey.
True Christian, baptised and confirmed . . .

I was born for sacrifice . . . the Sacrifice of my Christ.
I must continue and even fill up what is wanting here below in His Passion . . .

Throughout all my activities . . .

that is the sole important piece of work.
Then, why could I not pour all the activities of the twenty-
four hours of every day into the chalice?
And even with a single stroke, pour into it the rest of my year
and even . . .

all the remaining days of my life.
On this day of the nineteen hundred and fifty-first year since He began His Sacrifice . . .
"I will go in unto the altar of my God."

Judge me, O God! . . .

Judica me, Deus . . .
I want to be clean and pure before Thee.

Yesterday, at Thy feet, I received pardon for my faults. And
Thy Blood once again refreshed my soul . . .
Judge me while I am free from stain.
If the Saints declared themselves the worst of sinners . . .
if Saint Philip Neri thanked Thee, each evening, for not
having become a renegade during the day . . .
I can well give Thee thanks, myself, for not having been yester-
day or during these recent months,
such and such a bandit, such and such a swindler, such
and such a criminal mentioned in the papers . . . *ab
homine iniquo et doloso erue me.*
It is not through my own merit! It is by Thy Grace, my God!
From Thy Hand, I receive graces . . . and disgraces . . .
I accept everything . . . and all is well.

Then, why go I sorrowful?

Why this heaviness in recommencing today what I did yesterday? in putting my foot on the first of these steps? . . .
Ah, Lord, how well I realize that to the load of my faults is
added that of each day as it comes . . . begins and ends
. . . and begins again . . .
That daily cycle of boredom and routine . . .
must be overcome.
In this early morning hour, I need a push to carry me to
the crest of Thy holy mountain, my God.
Come, my soul! Wake up, shake off thy torpor; mount the
slope joyfully . . . take up thy march toward Love.
See! Above on the summit of the mountain bursts forth
the Light!

Emitte lucem tuam . . .

"Send forth Thy light . . .

and Thy truth . . ."

22

It is indeed they that have conducted me hither to Thy Tabernacle . . .

Send them to me, Lord!—

Thy light, to perceive clearly among the thousand human footpaths

Thine, the little "narrow way" where I shall surely meet Thee and where we shall together accomplish our Sacrifice;

Thy light, to discover the obscure way and the hidden door to . . . that soul . . . and that . . . and such another that I wish to gain for Thee this year;

and Thy truth, especially that enchanting truth:

that I am Thine . . .

that I am marked with Thy seal . . .

that I am a member of Thy Body, united under Thy Head with all my brothers and sisters, not only of my immediate family, but of all the world . . .

that I am Thine associate . . . in this Society of the Father, of the Son, and their common Spirit, of which Saint John speaks,

formed from all eternity on the Capital of Thy Blood, O Christ!

and which does not cease through the ages to atone for the sins of mankind.

It is indeed that truth of which I have just spoken . . .

truth which is light, which leads me today to the foot of this altar,

to cast my share into Thine Offertory . . .

that is to say every moment of this day which is beginning . . . already so heavy with sin . . .

O my God, give me a hunger and thirst for Thy light and Thy truth!

For Thou only art my strength.

Quia Tu es Deus, fortitudo mea . . .

Oh! how truly I feel it! . . .

If I possessed millions, I should be no richer, for my sole wealth
is in loving Thee and in having great love to give to the
members of Thy Body . . .

But Thou art the very fountain of Love.

Further, I must needs remember in the dawn of this new day,
that it is Thy strength which supports the world . . .

that it is Thy Finger that has just turned this page in the
great book of days . . .

and that in the weeks and months which are going to glide
away, I shall not make a movement or take a step unless
Thou bearest me up.

I want this ardent conviction . . .

that not a hair falls from our heads without Thy permission . . .

and that, in Thy Hand, emperors and dictators are as
pawns, as also am I, as also is the least little beast of field . . .

and that behind the curtain of appearances, Thou controllest, week by week, day by day, minute by minute, the
whole scenario of the universe,

and that nevertheless, for the Grand Drama of Love,

Thou claimest from Thy soldier: his two arms, his two feet, and
his whole soul, and his whole heart to its last beating.

Then, why not hope? . . .

Spera in Deo . . .

Why not proclaim Thee my Salvation and the Glory of my
countenance . . . and the Splendor of my life?

Why not, in spite of the dark outlook, let my heart be engulfed
in hope?

and why not go to Thine altar, to carry to Thee in advance, as a trophy, each hour of this day?

and again tomorrow, the next day, and always . . .

proclaiming that Thou art ever the Lord . . . the God of my

youth, who givest joy to my heart, who continually art restoring youth to the ages . . . making them more beautiful? . . .

Come, let us go forth!

Although I am fifty, sixty, or seventy years old, may my collaboration be every day more youthful and more fresh!

And may I say with renewed faith, with unwearied hope, with warm charity, these first words of the eternal Sacrifice, which is everlasting:

Introibo ad altare Dei . . . ad Deum qui laetificat juventutem meam . . .

I will go in unto the altar of my God . . .

of that God Who is the sole joy of my youth and of my life.

II

TO BE HUMBLE AND POOR

The Confiteor

And just as I have recited the psalm *Judica me* with the priest at the foot of the altar, with him also, and like him, I must say my *Confiteor;*

with him, and like him, I must strike my breast saying, "Through my fault . . . through my most grievous fault!"

Together we should show to each other a holy emulation of sincerity and purity.

Oh, Lord, make us understand clearly

that we cannot offer Thy Most Holy and Immaculate Host without having done our utmost to purify our souls, done all we can to make them a clean victim.

I trust sincerely that there is no barrier between Thee and me and that my soul is in a state of grace wholly unstained since my last absolution.

But there are a thousand particles of dust from the road:
>rudeness, self-love, uncontrolled words of the carnal and jealous man, little blotches on the soul from contact with others,
>specks of yesterday and of the day before and of this morning, carried along on the winds of luxury and of pride . . .

Oh, how necessary it is that I shake them off at the foot of Thy altar before Thine all-pure Majesty.

Confiteor . . .

And here . . . say the rubrics . . . the priest "makes his confession."
>In the presence of everybody, he confesses . . . he shows himself with his burden . . . he is not afraid to show himself thus.

And we see him incline profoundly because it is very heavy.

And he acknowledges it . . . and he asks that we have pity:
>"because I have sinned exceedingly" . . . and because of that, he seeks the intercession of the highest . . . and also the humblest:

Pray for me, O most pure Virgin Mary, O Saint Michael Archangel, O Saint John Baptist, O holy Apostles Peter and Paul . . . and you . . . my brethren . . .
>pray for the poor priest there, who feels all the weight of his flesh and of his spirit at the moment when he is going in to the altar of God.

O Priest, "who hast sinned exceedingly,"

yes, I will pray for you, but you must also pray for me . . .
>because I too have sinned . . . sinned exceedingly.

Before God . . . Oh! *there*, there is no dissimulation and boasting.
>No one is prouder than his neighbor.

26

We have all sinned.

There was even a time . . . during the early ages of the Mass . . . when, sustained by a holy fervor, each one—and the priest first of all—told his sins out loud, naming each one, so great was the candor and humility existing among them all, but . . .

the Church, mistress of discreet humility,

has willed that each individual should remain a nameless sinner before the others, reserving the precise names of his sins to the intimacy of Christ in the confessional.

But nothing prevents any one, O Lord, when he stands at the foot of the altar, from letting pass through his mind's eye in a lightning flash—as did the holy King David—the whole train of his misdeeds: his petty lies—his acts of injustice, of immodesty—his wrongdoings, little or great—in thought, word, deed, and omission . . . and there are so many! . . .

And if these were not enough to bear down his shoulders, there are the sins of his family . . . of his relatives and friends . . . there are the sins of those around him . . .

there are the sins of the city or of the village in which he lives, and of the whole country and of the whole nation . . . and of the world.

From the *Confiteor* on, the priest is a substitute.

O Christ, O my unique Priest, Thou didst take our place on the Cross.

O Christ of the first Mass, that day Thou didst draw down upon Thyself all my sins and the sins of all the world.

And it was laden with this immense weight, it was under this same burden that Thou didst expire.

So, Thy priests, in this unending Sacrifice of Thine, are substitutes as Thou . . . in commemoration of Thee.

The *Imitation* says truly that the priest goes up to the altar bearing on his chasuble two crosses: one in the front for his own sins, and the other on the back for the sins of others.

Sins . . . and their consequences . . .

O Lord Jesus, Thou hast included in Thy Sacrifice all sins . . . the sins of all mankind.

Thus, Thy priest at the altar, and all of us, *priests with him*, in Thee Who art the Christ-Priest, from this moment of the *Confiteor*, are all bound by the exigencies of your Sacrifice.

We must not only take upon ourselves the sins of others,

but we must also offer ourselves in expiation to the Justice of God . . . up to the end, we must substitute for other souls.

Lord, take me! Here I am! . . .

Take me for such a man . . . for such a woman . . .

They do not know Thee, or knowing Thee, they do not wish to love Thee . . . they do not wish to pray to Thee . . .

On the contrary, they are too much engrossed in dancing, love making, in cinemas, and cafes . . .

Many are still enchained by their passions . . .

Lord, I *must have* this soul . . . these souls . . .

Lord, I must have the salvation of my fellow workers . . .

I must have the salvation of my country . . .

It is for them all, that I am here . . .

for them all do I bend low that Thou mayest place upon *my* back the weight of the necessary reparation. But . . .

I fear . . . I dread Thy Justice.

I know that I shall have trouble enough to expiate my own sins.

What need have I to carry the burden of others when I am incapable of bearing my own?

Lord, grant me Thy light!

"Do not be afraid . . . it is *together*

28

that you carry the sins of your brethren.

There are millions of you to complete my Sacrifice . . .
millions to carry together my Cross . . . each has his own
little part in it, and the whole weight is shared by all.
I am well aware of what I have done. I have chosen you to
be the participants in my Priesthood . . .
It is I Who have placed in your heart this ardent longing
to pay the debt of the insolvent . . .

Well, be generous, offer yourself in participation . . . give
yourself in payment . . . be magnificent in your offering . . .

I will lay the rest to my charge."

Deus, tu conversus, vivificabis nos.

Lord, I understand. Only turn toward us with Thy strength and
Thy life . . . and Thy people will rejoice in Thee.
Lord, show us Thy mercy . . .
and let our cry go up to Thee.

After having thus joined with the people, in the verses and responses of this psalm of the most peaceful and pure confidence, forming but one heart and one mind with the
faithful who are present,

the priest prepares to mount the altar with his hallowed burden,

But he does not want to go alone . . .

III

DO NOT LEAVE ME ALONE

Reflections at the Dominus vobiscum

The Lord be with you!

Such is the first salutation of Thy priest, my God!
The congregaton will hear it eight times during the course
of the Mass.

29

Grant that it may be for us more than a mere form of greeting
. . . more than a *good morning* or an *adieu.*
In Christian countries, where Thy Presence is recognized, the
people bring Thee into their daily life . . . common greet-
ings of welcome and reunion . . . wishes for a safe voyage
and happy return!
In the fields of the Bible, those of Booz and Noemi, the master
saluted his husbandman thus: *Dominus vobiscum.*
And today, in the fields of Alsace, the people, making the Sign
of the Cross, say: "Praised be Jesus Christ . . . forever!"

Dominus vobiscum.

"The Lord," that is to say, the Father, the Son, and the Holy
Spirit:
may the Holy Trinity itself, present in this hallowed place,
be also in you, living tabernacles!
In each of you!
May God penetrate to the innermost fiber of your being; may
He be to you more than light, may He be fire!
O my dearly beloved brethren, the priest might say.
What could I wish you more glorious than that you may
be the luminous and glowing temple of the Father, Son,
and Holy Ghost!

Pax vobis! Peace be to you!

Such was the salutation of Christ on meeting His apostles along
the shore of the lake or on the roads of Galilee.
The bishop—because he is the visible representative of
Christ among us—repeats in the Mass the exact words of
Jesus.
Instead of *Dominus vobiscum,* he says, *Pax vobis.*
And so, the simplest formulas, the *bonjours* and the *bon soirs*
of the sacred liturgy, whether they are said by the bishop
or by a humble curate,

suppose the truth that God is always present . . . in us . . . among us . . . with His joy, with His peace.

There can be no life, truly Christian, without the presence and the sweetness of the "conversation" of God.

Four times during Mass the priest will turn around after having kissed the altar . . .

and say: *Dominus vobiscum.*

That is to say:

May this Christ Whom I love . . . at least Whom I so long to love . . . may this Christ Whom I have just embraced, press you also to His Heart.

O my brethren, let us love Him together . . .

Let us love Him so much that we will give Him not only our entire day, but our entire life!

And the priest makes an enveloping gesture which he intends to be all-embracing . . .

the gesture of the harvester who gathers to his heart the sheaf which he is about to bind.

Thus does he gather to his soul the souls of all who are present and who consent to be of one heart in loving God, present in their midst.

Et cum spiritu tuo,

they respond.

"May the Lord be in thy priestly soul."

May He be indeed its Master and one conquering Friend . . . We pray also that He will make of you the salt of the earth . . . the flame on the candlestick . . .

We need priests with burning zeal.

O you, baptised souls

who offer the Mass with the priest,

pray for your priests! Be mindful of the fact that in the Holy Sacrifice your every word has meaning.

31

A whole congregation saying, *Amen . . . Et cum spiritu tuo,*
  with fervor and faith . . .
  what a powerful breath on the hot coals!
  It depends on you to make them burst into flame!
At your prie-dieu, you need the fervor of the priest at the altar.
  At the altar, the priest needs the fervor of you at your prie-
  dieu.
There is but a single intensity of feeling throughout the chapel
  or throughout the great cathedral . . . a single expression
  of prayer and love.

Oremus: let us pray!

And so . . .
each *Dominus vobiscum* is to recall the attention, is an almost
  anguished insistence to prevent the prayer from being
  scattered.
  "The Lord be with you!" But you, my brethren, be with
  Me!
Please do not leave me alone . . .
  alone to pray . . . alone to love . . .
  alone to immolate Myself . . .
It is not alone the paten . . . It is not alone the chalice with the
  wine . . .
It is you, my dearly loved little ones, whom I wish to take hold
  of and lift up in my hands.

Oh, let us pray . . . let us pray together.

It is so important that we act as one!
  The end that we seek together is so mighty! . . .
  so majestic, the grace we pursue!
Let no one fail to be ready!
Let no one go off in a corner, jabbering and mumbling his own
  private prayers!
  The least among you . . .

the least and the poorest . . . I accept his prayer, for I
have need of it.
Individually, we have only our weaknesses and our impotence.
We must be dissolved and blended into one prayer,
living, breathing, and warm:

the prayer of Christ:

per Christum Dominum nostrum.
Thou hast said, O Christ,
"Where only two are gathered together in prayer, there
am I in the midst of them."
Oh! How Thou must hearken to us in the Mass . . .
And when Thou art present, present also is Thy Father, and
Thy Spirit . . .
The slightest breath, the tiniest sigh is perceived immedi-
ately and has weight in the Redemption.

O Father, so majestic and so loving . . .
abide with us . . .
and may our great task at Mass,
that of priests and of laity,
be to reunite in Him alone
Who is Thy well-beloved Son.

IV

THE KISS
TO THE SLEEPING CHRIST

The altar is Christ,

Altare, quidem . . . Ipse est Christus.
The Bishop thus informs the subdeacon, on the day of his ordi-
nation.
Further . . . palls and corporals are figures of the members of
Christ, that is to say: the faithful;

33

that is to say: all of you, my brethren, in my own land and
in the whole world.

You and I . . .
the altar . . . Christ!

The tomb of Christ asleep,

say the Holy Fathers . . .
where He will soon consent to be born again.

The five crosses engraved on the altar stone number exactly His
Wounds.

The bones of the martyrs encased therein, form part of the altar
and of His Body . . . as do I, as do we all.

The altar, however modest it may be, is Christ, and they are His
members in Him.

At the Mass, under the veil of these material mediocrities, is in
reality *THE ABYSS*.

The priest goes up to the altar . . .

Putting his foot on the first step, he says, "*Oremus* . . . Let us
pray!"

Let us pray that at the same time we may penetrate the
Mystery of this Holy Sacrifice, without sin . . .
that our hearts may be pure . . .

Let us pray that all priests, my brethren and I, may fulfill the
rites *nitide et diligentissime*, with all possible care and
exactness.

Let us pray that the glory of the Invisible may filter through
our poor humanity.

Let us pray that we may be the resplendent *screen* of God.

And as he approaches the altar,

he prays again, anxious at this moment to become perfectly
pure,
that the last traces of "his sins" may disappear . . . the

last little wrinkles which would veil in his soul the Beauty of God.

He cannot catch too much of the love of the saints, of their purity and of their ardor, of the ardor especially of the martyrs whose "relics are here"—*quorum reliquiae hic sunt.*

And he kisses the altar . . .

Just where the sacred relics rest:
the bones, never grown cold, of those who gave all their blood for Jesus Christ;
the relics, still glowing, of those first Christians . . .

As if it were still the time when Mass was being said in the Catacombs, on the palpitating body of the latest martyr!

As if, through this kiss, he would imbibe, poor priest, something of that "greater love" which consists in giving his life for Him Whom he loves!

To give his life . . .

Lord, I have spoken truly . . . for perhaps the time has come . . . to what time art Thou daily leading us? . . . to what day? . . . to what hour? . . .

The hour for the sowing? . . . The hour for the reaping? . . . The hour for the wine press? . . . Thine hour, that of Golgotha?

It matters little, O Christ, Thine hour will be mine! It is always the hour for a priest to be ready to give his life,

provided that I begin truly to love Thee . . . to be truly Thy disciple and Thy priest . . . provided that I live in the light of Thy Death for the souls Thou hast entrusted to me . . . provided that I die with Thee for them . . . when Thou wilt . . . where Thou wilt . . .

This ritual kiss . . .

and because it is ritual, awaited perfunctorily . . .
this kiss on the altar, is much richer than it appears; it can be
    cold, without relish and without tenderness.
        It is none the less holy, full of symbols, full of mystery and
        of deep-hidden meanings.
It is not only a mark of veneration to our brothers, the martyrs;
it is especially a greeting, it is a mark of love given daily to
    Jesus Christ, by the priest and all Christians.
It is the entire Church, His Spouse, who each morning, greets
    her Beloved, and repeats her vows . . .

                                        A love pact . . .

pledging of my day's work . . .
        of my whole being to Christ Jesus and to all our brethren
        in Him . . . feet, hands, lips, time, heart, to the service of
        the Blood of Christ worthy of bearing fruit in souls . . .
        today . . . and again tomorrow to begin once more!
A sign of the transport in which we deliver ourselves, lose our-
    selves in this labor of love!
And especially, the sign of a tenderness and a fidelity so loving
    that it will at length make reparation for the frightful kiss
    of him who betrayed!
And despite such mystic richness,

                                this kiss to the sleeping Christ

is only a sorry sign of human love.
But, because it is restored to health at the Source of love, it
    grows to infinity . . .
        It is less the sign of our love than the announcement of the
        great Love Who is coming.
        It is so little in what it gives, but so great in what it awaits.
It awaits the Son of God Who is about to be reborn in order to
    die again.
Of old, it was Mary, it was Saint John, who kissed the cross as

36

they waited for the Crucified to be let down into their
arms . . .

Now, it is the priest who kisses the place where he will soon
take into his hands the Body and the Blood of God.

This kiss of the priest on the altar . . . *is it not the foretaste
of Communion?*

Thus, the whole Church, priests and faithful, make haste each
morning toward the altar, as Magdalen on Easter morning
. . . irresistibly attracted by . . . LIFE.

Silently . . . mysteriously . . .

Apostles, Popes, Confessors, and Martyrs,
The Church triumphant and militant,
>   from all parts of heaven and earth,
>   the whole Church hastens to surround the altar . . .
>   It is the resistless ascent toward the Host.
And we, also, the privileged *faithful* carried along in the torrent,
the priest bearing our sins with his own . . .
>   his holy aspirations with ours,
>   our souls with his soul.
Oh! may he, while kissing the altar with attentive respect, say
to Him Who is coming,
Lord! Behold us! In this kiss, we have given our all; our body,
our soul, our life . . .
>   Thou hast only to accept them!

V

*EVERY MASS
HAS ITS DISTINCTIVE FEATURES*

From the Introit to the Gospel

Formerly, in the days of the magnificent High Masses, that of
the Pope, or of the Bishop and 10, 20, 30, 50, 100 priest con-
celebrants,

a splendid cortege moved from the sacristy to the altar:
bishops, clergy, servers with seven-branched candlesticks
of gold and silver;
then the Pope or the bishop who was to celebrate.
And while this procession was solemnly advancing through the
main aisle, men and boys of the *Schola* alternated in reciting the verses of a psalm . . . of a long psalm . . .
of a psalm that lasted as long as it took for the celebrant to
reach his prie-dieu, kneel, pray a few moments, and give
the signal for the *Gloria Patri.*
Such were, for nearly ten centuries, the majestic *Introits:*

worthy overtures to an enchanting Drama . . .

a sort of portal opened on a Mystery, like a triumphal arch at
the entrance to a Sacred Way, through which, amid the
rapture of the organs and the sparkling of the candles,
Thou comest to us, O Christ.
Now we live in the days of low Masses, and even Thy High
Masses seem to have little ceremony.
One verse, two verses, with the *Gloria Patri*, form the whole
Introit, recited in a low voice by the priest, or sung by a
few close associates.
Oh! how short it is, dear Lord! Oh! how silent!

But Thou hast willed it so . . .

through love . . .
through impatience to come often, to come every day,
not to cease one instant in coming to offer Thy Flesh and
Thy Blood,
It was not enough for Thee to have
one Mass in a big city every month . . . or every fort-
night . . . or every week.
Thou wilt have a Mass every minute,
a Mass in the most remote corners of the world,
not too long, not too short,

38

for the devotion of people harassed by the necessities of
    life.
And that is why Thou dost come now quickly, daily, intimately.
Thou dost come without ceremony, incognito, without brilliant
    lights, without resounding bells . . .
      with two little candles as lights, and . . . as music, only the
    little bell of the altar boy.

                        Blessed be Thou, O Master,

for this simplicity . . . this intimacy . . . this multiplicity . . .
But may I never have the misfortune,
    because Thou art frequent, to find Thee commonplace,
    because Thou art silent, to be deaf to Thee,
and because Thou comest in the early morning hours, five, six,
    or seven o'clock, may I not be so lazy as not to rise to re-
    ceive Thee.
Didst Thou not institute the low Mass in order that it might fit
    into my working day?

                 And because my soul also is a temple

more beautiful than this church, and more beautiful than Thy
    most beautiful cathedrals,
each low Mass must be a High Mass, for which I must myself
    furnish the lights and the plain chant.
The most resounding organs and the most brilliant torches
    do not equal in value, the simple desires,
    do not equal in value, the humble prayers of a lowly Chris-
    tian who offers himself to Christ.
The more so because . . .

                Thy least Words are precious,

as tiny parts of the Sacrifice . . .
and because I can say them all with the priest . . .
    Lord, grant that I do not lose one of them.
Before I receive the Host, I must receive Thy Word.

Before the Mass of Thy Flesh and Blood, there is the Mass of
     Thy Truth.
It is ever and always the *Mass of the Catechumens,*
          for who is not a catechumen . . . before Thy infinite
     Truth?

                         Thine *Introits* so reduced . . .

are so much the more vigorous and full.
They bring me, in selected verses, the spirit of this Mass.
They are the heralds of the Epistle and of the Gospel.
The whole tenor of the Mass is announced in them:
          and I know from the first syllables what state of mind I
          must bring to the Mystery, exalted or grave, rejoicing or
          mourning,
          always trusting, always loving.

                    For each Mass has its own countenance

and its spirit, in the never-failing fountain of the liturgy.
Introit, Collects, Epistle, Gospel, Offertory,
          determine each day, for the Christian, the attitude of his
          soul, its tone, its demeanor, its pitch:
a divine protocol which decides in what spirit we must offer
     our Host this day.

                              O Christ of this day,

it is indeed this very psalm; it is indeed this very verse;
it is indeed this very prayer that I must say today when going
     to meet Thee, is it not?
And how these texts, old as they are, can express my joy or
     my grief of this moment . . .
How this *Kyrie* and this *Gloria,* in their time-honored words,
     bear the sorrow and joys of this very minute!

                              Have mercy on us, O Lord.

Kyrie eleison! . . .

Have mercy on our coldness . . . on our routine.

Have mercy on our brothers and sisters who are suffering.

Have mercy on the war-torn countries, whose people are dying
because they do not have love.

Have mercy on this vacillating world! . . .

Have mercy on the peoples who will not agree . . .

Have mercy on everyone and everything . . .

O Father, O Son, O Holy Spirit,
what wilt Thou have from us?
what wilt Thou have from me today?

Gloria in excelsis Deo

Glory be to my God! Let me sing:
"Glory to God in the highest and peace on earth to men of
good will."

Let the song rise from us . . . who are not angels . . . nor yet
little shepherds . . .

What does it matter? We must say it to our friends, to our ac-
quaintances.

It is because men no longer say to God:
"We praise Thee, we bless Thee,
We adore Thee, we glorify Thee,"
that they hate and kill one another.

O Thou Who only art holy,

Who only art the Lord, the Most High, Who only art the
Priest,

O Thou Who hast exclusive control over the Priesthood and
over Love,

give to all who offer the Mass with Thee,
a share in Thy Secrets . . .
a share in Thy spirit . . .
a share in Thy devotedness and in Thy love.

VI

THE GOSPEL . . .
AND THE HOST

Gospel and Creed

"Lord, purify my heart . . .

and my lips, that I may worthily proclaim Thy holy Gospel."
I am not a preacher . . .
>I am a farmer, a lawyer, a doctor, a mariner, a student
>. . . or this . . . or that . . .
Still I must proclaim Thy Gospel.
My Baptism and my Confirmation give me a part in Thy priesthood . . .
>but they do not permit me to announce Thy Word in the
>Church.
But in the street . . . among my companions, at the workshop,
the office, the factory, the farms, the mine, or . . . at
home, at table, in the parlor . . .
>I can, I *must* proclaim Thy "good news" at least " as a
>fisherman on the shores of the lake,"
as Andrew, for example, who said to Peter,
>"Come and see the Messiah!"

O Christ, Who hast spoken so beautifully . . .

with the accent, the words, the expressions of Galilee . . .
>grant that my language . . . whether cultured or crude . . .
>and my accent . . . much more the accent of my heart
>than of my tongue . . .
may be a fitting garment for Thine august Truth.
O Thou, Who numberest every syllable that I pronounce,
>since Thou wilt demand an account at the Last Judg-
>ment . . .
>grant that none may be harmful, or even idle, today.

Grant that none may escape the service of Thy Majesty . . .
Grant that all my words may be Thy Word!
And even, I dare ask it of Thee, with Thy priests at the altar . . .
   grant that my lips may be pure and burning . . .
   like those of Thy great prophets . . .
   Why not . . .
and for greater surety . . . speak Thyself in me!
   Be Thyself in my heart and on my lips
that I may worthily and competently proclaim Thy Gospel . . .

                                    Thy Gospel,

that is to say, Thyself . . . what is immense, incomprehensible,
   unfathomable . . .
   in a Spirit which is God . . . in a Love which is God.
What is called "Thy eternal thoughts," "the secrets hidden
   from the angels . . ."
   the story of Thy kindness, Thy patience, Thy silence . . .
   all the divine mysteries, in human expression,
   in words that are ours . . . in words that are mine . . .
   is it possible?

                 We do not yet have Thy Flesh and Thy Blood,

but we already have Thy spirit . . . Thy Heart . . .
   which Thou dost pour out in advance, as a partial disburse-
   ment of the great treasure that is to come.
We cannot see Thee yet, but we hear Thee . . .
Thou art speaking from a distance, as if to say to us:
   "I am coming."
And thus I know that Thou art there, so near . . .

                   And when Thou art really here,

Thou wilt say to me nothing else than
   that Thou art meek and humble of heart . . . I know!
   that we must love one another . . . oh, yes!

and that if there be a preference, it should be for the poorest . . . I know indeed . . . but . . .
and that if one wishes to be great among his brethren, he
must throw himself at their feet . . . as Thou, Thyself,
wert at the feet of Judas.
There is not on one side, Thy Word . . . and on the other,
Thy Flesh and Blood;
The Word is inseparable from the Host . . .
the Gospel is the Word of God . . . under the letter,
the Host is the Word of God . . . under the bread,
and to hear Thee now is already to receive Thee.

Oh! may I receive Thee . . .

holily . . . eagerly . . . humbly . . .
May I hunger and thirst for Thee, O Word!
I must have as great an appetite to receive Thee in Word,
as to receive Thee in Sacrifice . . .
to comprehend Thee as to contain Thee . . .
Then, reveal to us Thy lofty conception of life . . .

Credo! . . .

Yes, to believe . . . I believe . . . we believe . . .
as the simple shepherds and the wise kings . . .
as the Samaritan and the centurion . . .
as Jairus and as she who said: "If I could but touch the
hem of His garment . . ."
Increase our Faith . . . Faith, in our minds! . . . and in our
lives . . . all our lives . . . that we may sing aloud with
heart and voice! . . . under the vault of cathedrals and
chapels, and also on the streets and in the market places . . .
that Thou art, O God, the All-powerful Creator,
that Thou art the well-beloved Son of the Father in Heaven . . .
and at the same time, the Son of Mary,
crucified at three o'clock on Good Friday . . .

whence, risen again and seated at the right hand of the Father . . .
Thou art all mildness and mercy to the needy and to the little ones . . .
that we may proclaim that Thou wilt return to take us with Thee . . .
and whilst we wait, Thou art there with us, in the confessional, and in our tabernacles . . .
and that we too are there . . .
we the baptised and confirmed, we the ordained . . .
forming with Thee but one body, one sacerdotal family . . . inseparable from Thy Passion, Thy Redemption, Thy Glory,
as much one in Thee as all the grains of flour pressed into the Host.
That is what I must believe . . . and *live*, even under trial and tears . . .
while . . .

I look for the resurrection of the dead—

Expecto resurrectionem mortuorum—and the life of the world to come . . .
Yes, I believe . . . already I have immolated myself in this Mass . . . casting from me, as one throws a handful of dust to the wind: prejudice, sham, sulkiness, vainglory, silly conceit; all this tinsel of my pride . . .
offering to Thee instead, in this Offertory, reason and understanding, imagination and affection, judgment and common sense, the most intricate workings of my mind—what I foolishly call my independence . . .
It is Thy Gospel which will take effect in me . . .
Thy Gospel condensed in the *Credo* so as to pierce souls . . .

It is Infinite Truth which will penetrate to the very core of my
    being . . .
    to impart to it all the fullness and all the strength . . .
    all the youth and
    all the charity of God.

The Total Offering of the Soul to Christ

From the Offertory to the Canon

The Total Offering of the Soul to Christ

From the Offertory to the Canon

To orientate your soul:

At this point, the non-baptised used to withdraw.

Only those could share in the Sacrifice who had received in Baptism "some share in the priesthood of Jesus Christ."

So, here begins the Sacrifice, and, with it, your effective participation. And as one does not truly participate in the Sacrifice without communicating, it is necessary now to prepare yourself for the Gift *par excellence*, the Host, by offering yourself. Christ must communicate with you before you communicate with Him.

Cast then, into this Offertory, the course at least of this day: your tiniest thoughts, words, and deeds for the next twenty-four hours. Add your tears, your sufferings, all that goes amiss in your life, all the drops of blood in your heart.

If you are humble and pure, if you have said your *Confiteor* sincerely, listened attentively to the Epistle and the Gospel, you will not admit any rapine in your holocaust. It is indeed the complete Christian who will present himself to the complete Christ, Christ of the Consecration, jealous of the glory of His

Father, Who gathers into Himself all creation *sive quae in terris, sive quae in coelis sunt* (Col. I, 19-20) and draws it into the fire of Sacrifice.

The priest has just said to you *Dominus vobiscum* to remind you that now is the time for you to heap upon the paten all the elements of the Sacrifice, the bread, the wine, all mankind, and the universe.

Do not miss the call.

Hasten humbly but whole-heartedly to make a total offering of yourself.

I

THE TOTAL OFFERING

The Offertory

> *Suscipe Sancte Pater, omnipotens aeterne Deus,*
> *hanc immaculatam hostiam . . .*

The priest raises the paten and the Host, and I say with Him:
"Receive, O Holy Father, Almighty and Eternal God, this spotless host . . ."
What! such a little thing for a God so powerful? . . .
and yet . . .
What is this mystery, that even before the Consecration, this morsel of bread is so heavy that it takes the extended hands of the entire Church to raise it up to God? . . .

Holy Father, Almighty and Eternal God,

Thou art terribly jealous!
Thou desirest to have everything . . . as if all were not Thine.
Thou desirest to receive everything as if Thou hadst need of it.
Not a grain of sand in the sea escapes Thine accounting!
Not a blade of grass on the earth!
Not a syllable from our lips!

50

Not a minute of our lives!
Not a beat of our hearts . . . which must not be offered
to Thee . . .
through the Hands of Thy Son . . .
through the Hands of our one Priest . . .
It was for that, He was sent upon earth . . .
in order that He might take the entire world into His arms
as a victim,
in order that He might make of it an Offertory which
would make a suitable return to Thy Glory and Thy Jealousy.
How heavy it is already . . .

the little host,

elevated between heaven and earth! I believe . . .
it is all creation: the harvests, the forests, the rocks, the oceans,
stars, the streets, the villages, and the cities,
. . . with the churches and the factories and the banks and the
great stores . . .
all this immense uproar which rises with its songs and
lamentations, its distress and its grumblings.
It is my brothers and sisters in Christ, with all their sighs, their
tears, their songs, and their prayers.
And it is my soul and body also . . . with all my thoughts,
words, and deeds during the course of this day.
And presently it will be the Body and the Blood of my Christ.
Ah! how truly Saint Paul says: *Omnia in Ipso constant*
(Col. 1, 17) "In Him all things hold together."
So, let nothing of my day be lost to Thy Glory, O Infinite
Majesty.
Let all pass through Thy Son up to Thee!
But, see! The priest lets fall . . .

a drop of water

into the wine . . . little insignificant fact! Yes! But . . .
  God *regards* a drop of water.
In the sight of Infinite Majesty, all creation . . . the world and
  all that is in the world . . . is nothing more . . . but all
  the same, it *is* a drop of water.
My day . . . a drop of water . . .
  and all that is in my day . . . walking, writing, sewing,
  conversation, music, sweeping, dusting; . . .
my day which falls into the chalice!
And behold . . .
  the drop of water becomes the wine . . .
  and the wine will become the Blood of God; the lightest
  beatings of my heart, the tiniest breath of my life, my life
  itself . . .
And I want it to fall there entirely, Oh!
  Take all!
Ineffable mystery! . . . Grant that by . . .

the mystery of this water and wine

. . . *hujus aquae et vini mysterium*
the splendor of Thy Divinity, the force of Thy Redemption,
  may be on my tiniest thoughts and on my tiniest deeds . . .
  that my day may be Thy Day, O Christ . . .
  that my life may be Thy Life . . .
  that Thy Sacrifice may be my sacrifice . . .
so that I may continue Thy Thanksgiving, Thy Expiation, Thy
  Adoration, Thy Imploration for the salvation of the world
  . . . in this corridor through which I am passing, at this
  table on which I am working, in this theater, in this bus, in
  this tram on which I am traveling.

Never before was I greater or smaller.

A drop of water . . . final and supreme expression of the universe . . .

52

And yet . . . I, a layman, I feel myself truly a priest here.

I add something to the Sacrifice.

I bear my host, to be a victim with The Victim.

Until the eleventh century, all the people formed in line at the Offertory, each one bearing his bread, his wine, his milk, his honey . . . a sacerdotal people going up to the altar of God.

Today, the oblation is motionless, silent and unseen, at my prie-dieu since I am a simple Christian . . .

simple, but great enough, powerful enough in my Baptism, to participate with my slightest acts "in the Divinity of Him Who has deigned to clothe Himself in our humanity, Jesus Christ, Our Lord . . ."

For our salvation and that of the entire world!

pro nostra et totius mundi salute!

What scope for my prayer henceforth! . . .

Because I shall be dissolved into Christ with all my day . . .

there is not one of my acts, there is not one of my steps that will not be for my soul and for all souls, a mint of salvation:

this household where peace does not reign . . . this sick person who shows no interest in Thee, O Christ,

this boy, this girl, who seek to amuse themselves . . . all the clients of the neighboring cinema . . .

all these disputes, national and international . . .

our brethren in the horrors of fratricidal war . . .

Receive, O Holy Father, Almighty and Eternal God, receive my humble day and all that is in it.

Receive my host . . . receive my last sigh and my life, that all these souls may love Thee, that at least in their last hour they may hunger and thirst for Thee, and that at last there may be on the earth, the great Joy and the great Peace of Thy Gospel.

II

RECEIVE US, LORD

*The Oblation of the Faithful
at the Holy Sacrifice*

The Offertory continues . . .

Offertory of the bread . . . Offertory of the wine . . .
> Oblation of the faithful: it is the same lifting up: it is the
> same rising of the world and souls toward God.
> Soon Christ, encircling within Himself heaven and earth,
> time and space, will pay homage to Infinite Majesty.

But . . .

shall I be accepted? . . .

How many times, during the course of the Sacrifice, the Church
> has us ask to be received by Thee, O Holy Father! There
> seems to be an anxiety hovering over our offering . . .
> will it be accepted?

Up to the very end, and even after the *Ite Missa est*, the priest
> keeps beseeching the Holy Trinity that our Sacrifice be
> acceptable: *Placeat tibi Sancta Trinitas.*

Certainly, O my God, Thou desirest our offerings . . .

Thou desirest them large, and copious, and entire . . .

Thou dost admit us, even us, simple Christians, to this incom-
> parable honor of adding something, not to the essential
> value of the Sacrifice, but to Its efficacy . . .

It is true, however, that Thou canst dispense with our gifts.

But we cannot dispense with giving.

There is no spiritual life without offering!

And that is why, every day at Thy Sacrifice, Thou wilt meet
> me again, Lord, as Thou didst meet my brothers and sisters
> of the primitive Church, bearing Thee the work of my

54

hands, of my mind, the bread and wine of my flesh and of
my blood, the milk and honey of my soul . . .
That is why hopefully . . . almost desperately, throughout the
course of my life, I shall continue to offer myself:

an Offertory which does not cease

to be received.
And Thou wishest me to know, O Lord, that the more one is
received, the more he must offer.
He must offer more in poverty and humility and contrition, in
the deep gratitude of the mendicant who *receives* all that
he is bound to *give*.
That is why the priest, in our place, inclines profoundly, his
hands joined on the edge of the altar, saying:

In a contrite and humble heart, receive us, Lord.

Us . . . and our sacrifice . . .
such is the rite of the "Oblation of the faithful" . . .
in spiritu humilitatis et animo contrito.
In order to say the Mass well,
to say a Mass which will be triumphant,
it is necessary that both priests and faithful, together,
should have said with deep contrition their *Confiteor*,
should together have recalled that they "had sinned exceedingly."
We have no hope of being acceptable
if we have this assurance,
this candid trust in our "character" . . . even spiritual.
Ah! how eagerly I shall make myself small enough to "pass
through the eye of the needle" . . . or at least under "the
low door" that leads to life.

Thus our sacrifice should be . . .

Et sic fiat sacrificium nostrum . . . ut placeat . . .

the only one pleasing to the Lord. Such is the eternal order of
the Sacrifice which succeeds:
to be mindful of our sins, to offer ourselves in expiatory sacrifice for the redemption of our associates, our intimates, our
family . . .
a victim humble and poor, and bruised already with compunction.
I bear to Thee, my God, my year, my day, my life. Wilt
Thou receive me?

Come, Sanctifier, Almighty and Eternal God . . .

Veni sanctificator omnipotens . . .
Surely the Holy Spirit must be mingled in our prayer.
Is not each Mass a marvelous continuation and a kind of
rebound of the Incarnation?
And should there not be in it a trace of Pentecost?
If all divine works are common to the Three Persons,
then the works of Love, the magnificently ingenious works
of Love, His prodigalities, through special "appropriation"
belong to the Holy Spirit.
This is indeed His special domain.
Is not the Mass, in last analysis, the supreme expression of the
Love of God?
Yesterday, today, Christ was born for me and then died
for my sins . . . and He continues . . .
We know, O Spirit of Love, that Mary conceived through Thy
operation, and that it is Thou Who, from her immaculate
flesh, formed the Body of Jesus.
When, in a short time, at the Consecration, the substance of the
bread and of the wine will yield place to the substance of
the Flesh and Blood of Jesus Christ, will it not also be Thy
sublime Travail?
We know, too, that until after the Ascension, the poor Apostles,

timid, human, weak . . . had no power to teach nations
and renew the face of the earth . . .
and that, actually, alas, we the witnesses of Christ, the apostles
of the present day, resemble them in a greater degree of
mediocrity . . .
And yet, O Spirit of Fire, Thy Pentecost inflamed them.
Peter and John rejoiced in being beaten.
Andrew ran to meet his cross, singing, *Salve, O Crux
speciosa*. "Hail, beloved cross!"
O Holy Spirit, dost Thou think that in those days of the primitive Church, Thy Pentecost came to an end?

O Sanctifier All-powerful

Thou Whom nothing can resist . . . come.
Thou Who completest masterpieces and Who dost inaugurate
them, plant in us the seed of goodness
and make it fructify!
We have no perseverance, no spirit, no fervor in offering ourselves with the Son of God.
We would like to leave Him and we, too, sleep while He is in
His agony.
What a big thing for us is an hour's prayer, a half-hour . . .
even ten minutes . . .
O Spirit of Initiative and of Great Persuasion . . .
arouse us all from our lethargy . . .
shake us out of our sloth and sweep us along . . .
quicken our souls to Prayer and Love!
And grant that through Thee, we, like Saint Andrew, may run
daily to our Sacrifice . . . our "beloved Immolation" . . .
and that, like Peter and John, we shall find delight in "having been judged worthy of being humiliated for the name
of Jesus."
O Thou, the Specialist of Love, and of the fresh bursting forth

of beauty in souls . . .

come . . .

and give to this Sacrifice prepared for Thy Glory, a luxuriant benediction!

And the priest, instrument of the Holy Spirit, blesses the offerings . . .

and it is time for the *Lavabo*.

In order that his whole being may be pure, he washes his hands, clean hands being only an emblem of total cleanliness.

Suscipe, Sancta Trinitas . . .

It is then in all confidence that he can say for us, "Receive, O Holy Trinity, this oblation which we make to Thee in remembrance of the Passion, Resurrection, and Ascension of Our Lord Jesus Christ . . ."

How can I really commemorate the Resurrection and the Ascension of Christ . . . if I am not myself a . . . *living memorial of the Passion?*

"Do this," He said to His Apostles . . . "in memory of Me!"

In order that we may truly "do this," that is to say . . . fulfill His Sacrifice in memory of Him,

I must bring to it the mind and the heart which He Himself brought to it on the eve of His Crucifixion.

I must resemble . . . in body and soul . . . Jesus Christ.

The Mass is all of one piece . . .

In spite of the several divisions and various fragments which appear on one trunk, like the successive graftings of preceding ages,

it is one single piece . . .

it is one single tree: the Cross

on which continually the salvation of the world is being accomplished by the immolation of Christ, and of His members in Him.

We shall be received unconditionally only if our sacrifice is
truly that: the Cross.
"Receive, O Holy Trinity, this offering which we make
to Thee, in memory of the Passion . . ."
and in honor of the Blessed Mary ever Virgin . . .
of Saint John the Baptist, of the Holy Apostles Peter and Paul,
and of the Martyrs (whose relics are here) and the Saints
whose feast we celebrate today, and of all the saints . . .
Here begins the gathering together of the Church Triumphant
around the Host . . .
More and more fully the Mass unrolls.
It is the *grande affaire* of Heaven and earth.
It is the Sacrifice of the *entire* Church.
All the Saints . . . and especially the most suited: Saint
John Baptist, Saint Peter, Saint Paul . . .
all their heavenly companions, with Mary at the head . . .
offer with us the Holy Sacrifice . . .
collaborate . . .
are material for the Offertory . . .
Think of it! . . .
The soul of the Immaculate Virgin there on the paten! . . .
and the heart of Saint Paul and of Saint Peter . . . and the
vigorous and loving faith of Saint John the Baptist . . .
At this moment in the Mass, there is at the altar a humble
priest, purified, sustained by the fervor of his brothers and sisters in Christ, who offer themselves with Him, and to whom is
added the incomparable reinforcement of the Virgin and of
the Saints. Even before the coming of Christ on the altar, what
hope of being accepted is given to us by this powerful concentration of all the forces of Prayer and Love before the gates
of God!

III

PRAY, MY BRETHREN

Orate Fratres

Orate . . .

A mighty offensive of Prayer is unlatched . . .

It is a pressing invitation, almost a command, that our priest gives to us, O Lord.

How can we fail to obey?

If there is any time which should be entirely PRAYER, it is indeed during Mass.

The Mass is not only a sacred prayer offered by us,

the Mass is . . . *P R A Y E R . . .*

the only prayer into which all the prayers of heaven and earth converge: breviary, rosary, ejaculatory prayers, songs of the angels and of the saints, which are only scraps, morsels . . .

of the one prayer which is . . .

that of Christ.

Oremus . . . Orate . . .

That is why the liturgy multiplies the repetition of the *Oremus*, of which the *Orate Fratres* is only a more pressing reminder.

The priest, at the altar, throughout his whole person: attitude, gestures and words, is the grand director of the prayer.

Firmly convinced that nothing can be accomplished without prayer, it is he who "collects" the prayers of all to mass them into one: that of Christ and of the Church.

It is he who after the prolonged moving about of the people, which in olden times was necessitated by the common offertory, turned again toward the faithful and said to them:

Peace! . . . Peace! . . . exterior and interior! . . .

Return now to your places! Enter again into your prayer . . .

Orate . . . We are going to penetrate into the very heart of the Mass.

"Brethren . . ."

For there must be present now *only* "brothers" and "sisters" in Christ . . .

No quarrels! no rancour! no bitterness among families, among classes.

There must be unity, for the full power of the Sacrifice!

Alas! O fraternity, O unity, O lost forces!

Every Sunday, in the sermon, the preacher says to us: "Brethren."

In every Mass, the priest turns around and says to us: *Orate fratres* . . . "Pray, brethren."

This salutation for many of us . . . for most of us, is colorless, savorless.

It passes unobserved, just a part of the sermon . . .

like a coin worn out from being dragged through everyone's pockets . . .

Christ, may every word of Thy Prayer have new meaning.

Christ, may Thy Mass become again

the Mass of the first Christians who had such love for one another, because they lived this brotherhood:

united in the single Prayer: Thine!

united in the single Host: Thine!

and consequently in the single Love which is: Thine!

and that, always and everywhere, in all places and in all stages of life.

God grant that some day these worm-eaten walls may fall . . .

all these palisades between classes, on which they placard their pride, their caste, their superiority . . .

No! . . . No! . . .

O Jesus, Thou hast said truly,
> "If you wish to be great among your brethren, make your-
> self the least of all."

Many of our young people: students, farmers, mariners, laborers, are forming themselves into a new knighthood to respect Christian women, to venerate them, and to love them
as sisters.

Employers, truly Christian, speak simply of "their brothers, the
Jocists."

The Jocists, for the past twenty years, have been sacrificing
themselves for their "brothers and sisters in Christ."

These practices and these words, O Christ, which come straight
from Thy Mass, are the first rays of a grand aurora.

> *. . . that my Sacrifice and yours . . .*

The joy of these words! . . .

Lord, Thy priest, our ordained brother, who represents us at
the altar, says to us in the name of the Church that his sacrifice is ours, then . . .
> let there be one single Sacrifice, one single Mass . . .

Whatever may be the meaning given to this word, "sacrifice,"
the offering is common, the Prayer, unanimous and fra-
ternal.

The Mass is not alone the Priest's.
> It is mine.
> It is ours.

The entire Church, in all its baptised members, has delegated
this priest to consecrate the Host.
> But once consecrated, we *all*, together, offer it to the In-
> finite Majesty of God!

> *Offerimus praeclarae Majestati tuae.*

It is we . . . It is our *gens sancta, regale sacerdotium.* It is
our holy race, our royal priesthood that does it.

We offer ourselves . . . we offer ourselves with the Host . . .
we offer ourselves together: men and women, angels and
saints.
It is a contest to find the most beautiful of gifts,
a contest to see who gives the most and the best:
a contest between the faithful there present . . .
a contest with the priest at the altar, our delegate . . .
and even, what folly! a contest with the celestial court,
with our Christ.
"The holy contention of love," Saint Francis de Sales called it.
Who will be the most generous?
Who will be the most merciless on his own inclinations?
Who will be the most empty of self?
Who will be the most lost in Christ?
in the stillness and lowliness of an offering which will soon fall
into the unfathomable gulf of the Consecration.

"Suscipiat . . . that our offerings may be presented
through your hands . . .

and accepted by the Lord, for the honor and the glory of His
Name, to our own benefit, and to that of all His holy
Church."
Thus, O Lord, dost Thou join . . . in part at least . . . the
glory of Thy Name and our sanctification and that of all
the Church . . .
to the gift which we make of ourselves, to the nobleness of
this gift.
Responsibility of Christians!
Appalling gravity of the Holy Sacrifice!
There is efficacy in this Sacrifice
in the measure in which I cooperate, that is to say, in which
I sacrifice myself,
and in which, with one accord, we joyously go on to the Consecration:

63

that is virtually to say:
to the death . . . of ourselves.
"Hail, beloved cross!"

> The sanctity of Catholic Action,

and its power to effect "the good of the whole Church";
the sanctity of its promoters . . . beginning with priests . . .
    depends on the manner in which they say the Mass and live
    their Sacrifice.
My God, may the enthusiasm of this total offering not be weak-
    ened in souls!
May it become more ardent, on the contrary, every day, at
    every Mass.
    Catholic Action will be what its enthusiasm for the Sacrifice
    will be.
From a lukewarm enthusiasm will come forth:
    not the city of God . . .
    but an enterprise of bluff and show, placards and photog-
    raphy.
The most ardent promoter will be ensnared by the very role he
    is playing unless he immolates himself . . . truly.
Unless each day, at the Consecration, he crushes his ego,
    will carry off the victory, will triumph on the conference
    and over convention platform . . . and finally . . .
    will kill his zeal.

> O Brethren, let us pray

that our sacrifice may be indeed a Sacrifice, that is to say:
    a sincere immolation of ourselves,
    a consecration of our whole being to the *grande affaire*
    of Jesus Christ.

IV

THE FIRST CHORDS
OF THE GRAND EUCHARISTIC SYMPHONY

The Preface

The common Preface . . .

A preface . . .

a musical prelude . . . an overture . . .

to the grand symphony of the Angels . . . as once at Bethlehem, to celebrate the coming of the New-born!

An invitation to prostrate ourselves in grateful adoration before a Host which will soon be living!

A prologue to the most beautiful drama of love that will ever be known, on the scene of which I am about to enter . . .

They are waiting for me . . . I must prepare my soul . . .

And . . . already! . . . the first splendors of the Radiant Well-beloved are coming from the distance . . . as if to say to us . . .

Attention! . . . I am coming . . . in a few minutes, I shall be with you!

with all the angels and all the saints . . .

The first chords . . . the first outburst of our thanksgiving, of our Eucharist joys, *because He is very near . . . because soon He will be at our disposal!*

But then . . . how our brothers and our sisters, the first Christians, made this dialogue vibrate with love!

Per omnia saecula saeculorum . . .

Amen.

Yes! forever and ever may it be thus.

O priest, who art at the altar in our stead, may the Lord be with you and with us . . . and may we be eternally one with Him in our homage and in our prayer!

Dominus vobiscum. Et cum spiritu tuo . . .

As the great mystery of the plenitude of God approaches . . .
>how important it is that we cut away the last cables that
>bind us . . .
>The priest says . . .

>>>*Sursum corda: Lift up your hearts!*

Our hearts? . . . But we have already lifted them on high.
>We have just cast them into your Offertory.
>You have taken them on the paten.
>You have offered them to the Father all-powerful, with
>arms extended.

Our hearts? . . . But they already belong to the Lord.
>Then . . .

>>*Gratias agamus Domino Deo nostro . . .*

"Let us give thanks to the Lord our God."
And the people decisively agree:
>"It is meet and just."
>And the priest takes it up again:
>"It is truly meet and just, right and availing unto salvation
>that we should at all times and in all places, give thanks
>unto Thee, O holy Lord, Father Almighty and Everlasting
>God . . ."

In the light of Thy holy spirit, let us reflect . . .
For such a grace . . .
>the grace of Thine unending Sacrifice . . .
>the grace of having there on the altar, Thy Flesh and Thy
>Blood, Thy Body crucified . . . soon to be within us . . .
>to continue with Thee Thy passion . . .

Ah, truly, Thou art deserving of thanks!

>>>*at all times and in all places . . .*

semper et ubique . . .

not only in the church, nor at our prie-dieu at home,

66

but also in the street, in the shops, in the office, at the factory, in the fields, in the market, in the theater, the train, the bus, on the open sea, on ship, at tennis, at the cinema, in the parlor, and even at the ball . . .

at all times and in all places.

"Nothing is more just and right." In fact . . .

O God, Our Father,

Thou laborest unceasingly . . .

and Thy Son likewise . . . ceaselessly the Redemption is being carried on.

It will continue as long as the earth shall revolve.

To the right . . . to the left . . . before me . . . behind me . . . wherever I go . . . there are souls to win . . . to save . . . to love . . .

And for these, at each second, throughout the world Hosts are rising up.

O Father, in a couple of minutes, Thy Son will be on the altar. And in an hour, or two, or three . . . it will be the same! "Christ's agony continues until the end of time," says Pascal.

At all times and in all places . . . true!

Such is the absorbing drama which is being enacted behind the curtain.

The Mass is always going on.

The Consecration is continually being celebrated.

There is no cessation of the unfathomable "Mystery of Faith."

The Eucharist, then, that is to say, Thanksgiving, is continual.

But how can this be, Lord? How dost Thou wish us to thank Thee at all times?

We are so pressed for time!

Per Christum Dominum nostrum.

"Through Christ Our Lord . . ." through Me, the Christ of the Mass.

67

It is impossible for you, yourself, to sing all day long the praises of My Father . . . with a book, a pen in hand, or at the typewriter . . .

It is impossible to reach to the Father . . . except through Me!

It is then, O Christ, Thou Who takest upon Thyself the duty of our thanksgiving.

It is Thou Who at every hour of the day and night givest to the Father, the sole Eucharist, the sole Adoration, sufficient and full.

And in a minute now, Thou wilt have delayed not a second before Thou wilt have taken our whole day's toil,

which already Thou wilt have bathed in Thy Love, to offer homage to the Infinite Majesty.

With what full hearts, then, must we sing this Preface which leads the way to the perfect and complete Eucharist . . . the Thanksgiving given every moment and in every last corner of the world.

Per Christum Dominum nostrum.

Per quem Majestatem tuam laudant angeli.

"Through whom the angels praise Thy Majesty . . ."

O holy angels, so magnificent . . . so subtle, so heavenly, you are no better able than we to give praise to God.

And the Dominations no more, when it comes to adoring Him.

And the Powers, when their veneration trembles with love before Him.

And the Virtues of Heaven and the Seraphim, when they wish to unite their transports to celebrate His Glory . . .

All the harps and the viols and the flutes and the hautboys and the tambourines which Fra Angelico placed in the hands of his angels cannot make heaven vibrate with love and harmony . . .

unless Christ, as Master of the Choir, gives the signal which gathers into one single soul, HIS OWN, these millions of angelic souls, playing . . . and celebrating in transports of rapture and love . . .

the radiant and glorious Beauty of the Infinite Majesty.

With whom we pray Thee join our voices also . . .

Cum quibus et nostras voces . . .

O God, our Father, grant that we may play our little part in this grand concert: soprano, tenor or bass, alto or contralto, according to our talent.

Lord, give us, henceforth, a little place in the brilliant orchestra of Thy angels and saints.

And in spite of all the din here on earth—whistles, motor horns, rumblings and groanings from political and labor disputes— grant that our ears may be attuned to hear this immense symphony which fills heaven and earth . . . and of which Thy Son is the grand Inspiration and the Rhythm and the Sovereign Measure.

Oh, that we may be so put out of conceit with the sound of our own voices that never more shall we consent to pray alone . . .

On the contrary, let us unite with Christ, and in Him, with all His members in heaven and on earth.

Let all our *Aves* and *Paters* and *Glorias*, all our tiniest aspirations and prayers be cast into the whirlpool of harmony which encircles heaven and earth.

That all together . . . above and below . . . North, South, East, West . . .

all the angels and the saints . . .

and the canons in the cathedrals singing the Office,

and the priests reciting their breviary,

and the monks and nuns in their monasteries,

and we ourselves, attending to our daily duties, trivial howso- ever they be, may all sing aloud with and through Christ:

Holy, Holy, Holy, Lord God of Hosts . . .
"Holy . . . thrice holy, the God of armies.
Blessed is He who cometh in the name of the Lord."
Let us sing! Let us make melody in our hearts!
For soon, we must be silent and lose ourselves totally in Him.

The Total Immolation

From the "Te igitur" to the "Pater"

The Total Immolation

From the "Te igitur" to the "Pater"

To orientate your soul:

The Offertory has already prepared you for the Consecration. The Canon is a further preparation and a protection. It completes in you the despoiling of "him who is not," in order that you may receive "Him Who IS." It is the grand, silent clearing away to allow Christ to enter fully into you and to permit Him to take full possession.

In deep recollection, then, after you have meditated on them, follow all the prayers that the priest says in the name of all, and as they gradually unroll, pray first for the Pope, the Bishops, for your brethren in Christ.

Enter into communion with the whole Church: that of ancient times, that of the present day, that of Heaven and of earth . . . with Her, with Christ, deliver yourself body and soul to the Infinite Majesty and supplicate Him to receive you with His Son . . .

Then, have a hunger and thirst for Him. Wait humbly till He comes forth from the Bosom of the Father . . . more beautiful still, and all flowing with graces and blessings.

THE CANON

> Realm of mystery and of silence surrounding
> the Consecration . . .

The Rule . . . in Greek: Canon . . .
  this piece of wood on our desks, which we take in our
  hands, lay it flat on our pages and let the pen follow *in-
  flexibly* . . .
  to draw a line, make an underscoring . . .
The Rule . . . an unbreakable formula, inflexible also . . .
  an order prescribed for the Consecration.
  It is *ne varietur*. It may no longer be changed.
Once, they spoke of the "Action" or "the breaking of bread,"
  or again "the Prayer—the Canonical Prayer."
  Action, the most sacred, since it is:
  the Miracle of the bread and wine changed into the Body
  and Blood of Jesus Christ.
  Prayer, the most august . . . the Infallible Prayer, since it
  always obtains what it asks:
  the Good *par excellence*, the light and the salvation of nations, the presence on the altar . . . of Christ the Saviour.
He is coming . . . The solemn moment is approaching . . .
After the lyrical effusions of the *Sanctus*, there is now necessary . . .

> profound recollection.

Up to the fifth century, the priest recited the Canon aloud.
  In the centuries that followed,
  It was sometimes aloud, sometimes in a whisper.
The Holy Council of Trent definitively sanctioned this mys-
  terious silence around the words of tremendous import.

The Church, mistress of her discipline and her liturgy, invites
priests and faithful to *profound recollection*.
She wishes, without imposing the complete isolation of the
ciborium and the drawing of the silken curtains over the
Sanctuary, that at least *souls should retire into themselves*,
and that the priest should enter into the "Mystery of
Faith" as the High Priest of the old law into the Holy of
Holies,
or rather, as the Saviour, into the Cenacle, to celebrate the
Last Supper.
Around the Holy Consecration,
the Church sets up this great zone of mystery which con-
tinues from the *Te igitur* to the *Pater*.

O Jesus of the Consecration, make Thy faithful,
particularly Thy choir directors, understand . . .

the ineffable value of silence:
and of that especially which permits the plunging of the
entire soul into the most profound of Mysteries.
O you, who are the leader of divine lauds,
you have the noble mission . . . almost the vocation,
of teaching people
to sing here on earth the *Gloria* of Heaven,
and of leading them on, meanwhile
through the suppliant *Kyrie*
to the resounding *Credo*.
It is for this reason that you have received
the fingers of a virtuoso
and the divine gifts of rhythm, measure, and voice.
But if you could understand . . . oh! . . . how grateful we
priests would be!
if you could understand . . . that even at High Mass, and
with all the more reason at low Mass . . .
there is a time to sing and a time not to sing,

and that there are in the course of time, certain instants that are
sacred . . . matchless, during which we should adore in
silence,
and during which the hush of your music would be more
beautiful, a thousand times more beautiful than your song.
At three o'clock on the afternoon of Good Friday,
all the Jocists stop in the midst of their work, lay down their
tools, and venerate in silence this minute during which, two
thousand years ago, Christ rendered up His last sigh on the
Cross, for us.
Is there really anything else which matters, in the past, in the
present, or in the future?
Then, PLEASE, every day, at Mass,
during the few minutes of the Canon,
let us *renounce everything* in order to adore Christ, Who
is immolating Himself for us and pressing us to do likewise.

II

*THEREFORE WE HUMBLY BEG AND
BESEECH THEE, MOST MERCIFUL FATHER*

Te igitur, clementissime pater . . .

It is indeed true, then!
I may come to Thee every morning, most Merciful Father!
O Father full of meekness and tenderness,
in spite of Thy majesty . . .

I have, therefore, the joy . . .

of presenting myself before Thee, fearlessly and confidently
because it is Thy Son who presents me . . . *per Christum
Dominum nostrum.*

He, Himself, has told me in His Gospel;

76

Saint Paul, the great Apostle, has told me:
> there is no Advocate more occupied, *Semper interpellans pro nobis* . . .
> "He ceaselessly intercedes for us";

there is no Gate-keeper more busy, *Nemo venit ad Patrem nisi per me* . . .
> Throughout all the ages, mankind will pass through Him.
> Nay more . . .

He is at the same time the tool and the function.
> He is Himself the Gate.
> He is Himself the password.

    O Father most merciful, this password is mine!

Dost Thou not recognize my voice?
> This Gate . . . is mine . . . Dost Thou know . . .
> this mendicant who is always knocking? . . .

Let me humbly beg permission
> to pass immediately . . .
> not to wait for months and years . . .
> For I have been waiting for years . . . for ages . . .
> Dost Thou not recognize Thy poor Lazarus?

Let me beg Thee humbly
> that this Mass may be . . . *the* good one
> the one in which I shall love Thee to the point of giving
> all to Thee, like Thy Son, like all the Saints.
> Lord, will it be this time?

        Now we enter into

the very heart of the great Mystery of Love . . .
> It is a solemn moment.
> United with one another and fused into Christ,
> Let us close ranks! Let us become powerful.

      But let us follow the Canon!

Let us conform to the Rule!

The Mass means that we must become one with Christ and all our brethren in Him . . . in the Mass we must forget our individuality.

We must put off our stage character completely: the "I," the "we," the "thine," the "mine,"

and then, without sight, without sound . . .

plunge into the Abyss . . .

AND LOSE OURSELVES IN HIM.

III

ALL . . . FOR THE SACRIFICE
"HAEC DONA, HAEC MUNERA . . .
HAEC SANCTA SACRIFICIA . . ."

These gifts, these presents . . .

which no soiled hand has touched . . .
as these words have already proclaimed . . .

have already invoked . . .

"the pure Host, holy Host, unspotted Host" . . .

Hostiam puram, Hostiam sanctam, Hostiam immaculatam . . .

All these prayers included in the Canon

are one with the Consecration.

It is one and the same sacred moment!

one and the same august Silence, and one and the same Adoration!

Christ is so near that already the species are being illumined, and by a holy anticipation, the Church bids us reverence them . . .

Three times the priest blesses them, then says again the words of the Offertory:

Offerimus
"O Father, together, we offer them to Thee! Receive them!
Bless them! We conjure Thee . . .
Supplices rogamus ac petimus.
Always the same agonizing cry to be accepted! . . .

                                 But among these presents and these gifts

ready for the Sacrifice . . . objects already sacrificed . . .
    besides this bread and this wine which will soon be Thy
    Substance,
    is there any of *our* substance?
    is there any of *our* being?
My God, everything that I cast into Thy Offertory was indeed
    for the Sacrifice.
And behold the moment of execution has come.

                                        It is momentous!

I have laid everything there; my whole heart is at Thy dis-
    posal . . .
    all my wealth . . . if I have any . . .
    all my health . . . that is to say, my life.
Intending, at least I hope so, to take nothing back,
    I am resolved that if Thou callest me today,
    I will not cling to anything,
    not to my money, nor to my valuables, nor to my business,
    nor to my family . . .
    I will say to Thee: "Take me! According to Thy Will!"
I have laid there on the table of Sacrifice
    my whole self, sensual and proud:
    my greediness, my idleness, my irritability, my curiosities
    in reading, my unguarded looks . . .
    all these silly roots of vanity, of pride, and of voluptuous-
    ness, which push themselves up between the pavements of
    our streets, through the crevices in the waxed floors of our
    drawing-rooms:

egoistic platitudes . . . vain mediocrities.

I am determined to throw them all into the fire, like dry grass,
like so much old paper.

I will take nothing back . . . *haec dona* . . . *haec munera.*

O Christ, what irony! *I* make *Thee* a gift!

And Thou art indeed ready to accept it . . . Nay more!

Thy delight . . .

is to be in the midst of it all . . . in this turmoil . . .

is to be born on our straw,
that of Bethlehem . . . or of Paris . . . or anywhere
else . . .
whether it be immaculate . . . or untidy . . .

What does it matter? Thou blessest our offerings,
Thou purifiest them . . .
Thy Beauty shines forth in them.

In a minute, the fire,

the Fire of Thy Spirit will consume all the substances,
and there will be . . . O marvelous reformation! gold under the ashes.

Just as under the bread and under the wine
will be Thy Flesh and Thy Blood,
under my tiniest actions henceforth . . . under my deeds,
most humbly offered, will be Thy Adoration, Thy Thanksgiving, Thy Expiation, Thy Imploration.

This indifferent, apathetic being that I was . . .

this sensitive, conceited, irritable person that I am . . .
will make triumphant efforts
with sweetness and humility,
with simple courage and purity,

that through the multiple woof of my life may appear the one
thing to be done:
the grand Work of Salvation through Love,

immolation with Christ immolated!

in a word:

TO LOSE MYSELF IN HIM WITHOUT DESIRE OF
RESTORATION

If . . . not . . .

If, after offertories and Consecrations without number, my associates find me the same: vain and sarcastic, ready for any
pleasure, snatching at every bagatelle . . .

they will say, with all reason, that this enthusiasm forms but a
part of my costume, and that I appear on the scene like the
Pharisee, arms laden with offerings, but with empty words,
thirsting for notice, and thoroughly disgusting with pride.

Everything is there . . . except the Sacrifice . . .

The Pharisee loses nothing of what he offers . . .

In his two clenched fists, he holds all that He offers Thee.

O Lord Jesus, Thou Who hast instituted the Holy Consecration,

in order that I might be present at the Cross, in spite of the two
thousand years that have passed, do not permit this to be a
vain parade. Grant, on the contrary, that I may fulfill my
sacrifice ritually, holily, sacerdotally,

losing myself, soul and body, in Christ,

for the Church, first of all

and for all the souls that I am bound to save.

IV

IN THE FIRST PLACE,
FOR THY HOLY CATHOLIC CHURCH

Imprimis pro ecclesia tua sancta Catholica . . .

1.

In order that she may be youthful and fresh . . .

The first! *Imprimis!* . . .

First in Love . . .

> because the Church . . . is the Mother!
>
> because the Church . . . is the Spouse!

We *could* dissemble . . . not give our best . . .

> . . . that would be so much according to our inclina-
> tion . . . and think first of all
>
> of "me," of "us,"
>
> of "Louis, Jack, Matilda, Cunegund . . ."
>
> of "the examination of this one, the grippe of that one . . ."
>
> of "the betrothal, of the marriage of this girl or boy."

But No! No!

We must pray *first* of all for "our Holy Mother the Church."

And if, yielding to the inclinations of an inveterate egotism,

> we clip off the edge of the gift . . .
>
> counting and weighing our goods, as a merchant in his
> booth,

O Christ of the vendors in the Temple, do not hesitate!

> I pray Thee, in a burst of holy passion for Thy Church,
>
> upset our counting tables,
>
> snatch from our hands our silly balances,
>
> go straight to the bottom of our hidden recesses,
>
> and cast *all* our reserves at the feet of Thy Well-beloved!

At the moment when we should relinquish all . . .

> what are these miserable things to which we cling?

Thou, O Father, didst not act thus!

> Thou hast so loved the Church . . .

that Thou hast given Thy Son . . .

> "The only-begotten" . . . which means . . . all.

And Thou gavest Him without reserve . . .

> (with the right to use or abuse)
>
> that He might be her hostage and her victim;

in order that she might be . . . she with Him . . .

> all-powerful against Thee,

irresistible before Thy Justice and Thy Love.
Then, how dost Thou put up with our meannesses, our bargain-
ings, and our withdrawals?
Come, my soul! Your gift must be entire! . . .
Thou, Thyself, O Christ, hast so loved the Church . . .
that Thou hast delivered Thyself entirely for her,
in order that Thou mightest offer to Thyself this spectacle—
ut exhiberet sibi—of a glorious Company without spot or
wrinkle: *Gloriosam Ecclesiam non habentem maculam,
aut rugam aut aliquid hujusmodi* (Eph. V, 25-27).
A Church, not mediocre . . .
not listless, not neglected . . .
not comfortably set up in appearance . . .
that, or something approaching it *aut aliquid hujusmodi,*
but a Church, on the contrary,
strong in its youthful countenance,
sparkling in its purity,
eager for the task ahead.
O Christ, in the hope of this joy, what hast Thou not done?
Thou hast delivered Thyself entirely . . . *Haec dona,
haec munera.*
And Thou ceasest not to deliver Thyself.
In half a minute, Thou wilt be there, on the altar,
THE DELIVERED, THE ABANDONED, THE CON-
SECRATED.
How can we fail to be with Thee? . . . and . . .

entirely for all the Church . . .

Yes, Lord . . . all.
What a fine opportunity to escape from ourselves! from these
few square inches comprised in our height and width! and
those extensions of ourselves:
those nice little air-tight circles in which we cuddle ourselves:
circles of family . . . or of rank . . . or of business . . .

or even of parish or of country . . . oh! yes, little circles!
when it is the whole Church that we should embrace in our
    prayer . . .
when it is the whole Church that is imploring peace, union.
Ah! Let us get out, I beg you! Let us take the air!
    Let us expand our lungs and take a deep breath in the open
    country!

2.

That there may be one fold . . .

Not long ago . . . brothers were killing one another in Spain!
Of late, French, Germans, English . . . again, brothers were
    killing one another!
    O Christ! It is Thy Church which is bleeding!
But . . . without machine guns, without rifles, without cannon
    . . . can brothers not fight one another?
    for example: sully the reputation of one another, bespatter
    another's name, offend one another in thought or deed
    . . . enrage one another . . . and finally destroy one an-
    other in the esteem and in the hearts of others?
How many Christians kill one another thus?
    How many families? How many newspapers? How many
    political parties?
    And it is Thy Church which is bleeding . . .

Lord, we beseech Thee! . . .

Peace for Thy holy Church!
We give Thee all for that: *Haec dona, haec munera* . . .
Please, let it no longer be said that the wolves alone agree . . .
    to devour . . . and the pickpockets to steal.

Peace! . . . Peace! . . .
Union! . . . Union! . . .

How I should love to have heard Thee pronounce this word, O
 Christ!
With what stress of voice Thou saidst and resaidst it, "after
 taking bread."
Saint John, Thy beloved Apostle, understood it and repeated it
 with Thee unceasingly: "That they may be one! . . . that
 they may be one! . . .
 O Father, that they may be one as we are one." (John
 XVII, 21).
In Us . . . that is to say:
that they may be melted into, dissolved in Thy Love! . . .
 that Love which is Thy Spirit . . . that immense Love
 with which Thy Son loves Thee . . .
O most holy and most loving Trinity . . .
 all these separate churches scattered in the fog and in the
 cold:
 in France, in England, in Germany, in Russia, in America,
 in China:
 embrace them . . . reassemble them! . . .
How often Thou didst long to do it . . . without our willing
 it . . .
 *Quoties volui congregare . . . quemadmodum gallina . . .
 et noluisti* . . . (Mtt. XXIII, 37).
Today many wish it with all their soul and give their all for it.
 Reassemble all Thy little ones, *filioli mei*, under Thy
 great wings!
Thou Who hast created families and countries . . . when, then
 . . . in reverence to families and countries . . . wilt Thou
 bring about the universal brotherhood of Thy Church?
 Haec dona, haec munera . . . We give Thee all for that.
How long wilt Thou allow us to pass
 "as poets and dreamers," desiring it zealously . . .
Why hast Thou given all Thy Blood and all Thy Masses . . .
THE ONE FOLD UNDER ONE SHEPHERD.

3

Under One Shepherd

Our Holy Father Pope Pius XII . . .

Whether he be Pius IX, Pius X, Pius XI, or Pius XII;
whether he be Leo XIII or Benedict XV . . .
   the Pope is the one Shepherd.
   He is Christ.
For him, in earlier times, that is to say for Thee, O Christ, and
   for Thy Holy Church,
   our ancestors in France, Ireland, Italy, Austria . . . gave
   their blood and their lives.
Today we are asked only for the immolation of our *mind* . . .
   Do we hesitate!
Let each of Thy Encyclicals, O Christ!
   Casti connubii, Rerum Novarum, Quadragesimo Anno,
   Divini Redemptoris, Summi Pontificatus . . . be a field of
   battle . . . on which Thou wilt triumph over us . . . over
   our selfishness, our indifference, our apathy, our worldly
   mentality.
   After all, You must take us as we are.
The main point is to surrender ourselves daily . . .
   haec dona . . . haec munera . . . for our Holy Father
   Pope Pius XII . . .

and our Bishop,

for him who binds us to the Pope . . .
and the bishops, also, of the entire world, those who, united
   with the Pope and with Christ, together "rule the Holy
   Church of God."
With what veneration and what love must we regard our Bishop
   and obey him! as one of the links of this living chain,
   riveted to the throne of God:

Christ, the Pope, the bishop, and we ourselves: priests and faithful and God Who holds the two ends of the chain.

Our pastor . . . with his curates . . .

who binds us to our bishop . . .
our priests who are there each day in His Name, our representatives, our witnesses . . . at the altar, when they take up the Host,
in the pulpit, when they announce the Word . . .
O Lord, may we act as one!
And may their Offertory and their *Dominus vobiscum* embrace us all and stir us up.
Being united with them in prayer, may we be united also in action,
so that when they say, "these good Shepherds," "Let us run after the lost sheep!" we shall run.
And when, after having run a long course, they say to us, of this wandering sheep: "See! there below . . . at the bottom of the ravine . . . and already my soutane is in tatters! Go . . ."
we shall go immediately through brambles and rocks . . . young and strong . . . to reclaim "this poor boy" . . . "this poor girl" . . . who has been led astray by the charm of music and of love.
Oh! What need we all have, dear Lord, of the same Bread and of the same Mass!
Imprimis. It may well be our great . . . our primary intention: the Holy Catholic Church . . .
May the faithful act in union with their pastor.
May the pastors act in union with their bishop,
May the bishops act in union with the Pope.
May the Pope act in union with Christ.
And the great city of souls will mount higher and higher to Heaven

with which it will be fused . . .

blessed and radiant vision of peace.

Let us pray for Our Holy Father the Pope and for our

bishops and priests . . .

O our Christ, Thou Who didst call to Thyself Thine apostles,
continue to call Thy bishops and priests.

Let them not make choice of themselves! But do Thou choose
them!

non vos me elegistis sed ego (John XV, 16) . . .

Call them on the border of the lake and in the fields! . . . at
the cash windows of our banks . . . among masters or em-
ployees or laborers . . . where Thou wilt! provided that
they hear Thee say forcefully, "Follow Me!"

Nourish them with Thy pure doctrine and with the marrow of
Thy great Heart . . . with Thy energy, with Thy boldness, and with Thy wisdom.

Press them with Thy spirit,

that they may enclose themselves in the Cenacle with
Mary;

that they may cast themselves in the water, like Saint
Peter;

that they all may be Thy well-beloved, like Saint John;

that they may walk amongst the little ones, like Thee;

that, being little and poor themselves, they may have Thy secrets revealed to them;

that their business sense may never stifle their love;

that they may salute their cross, like Saint Andrew;

that each day they may lose themselves in Thy Holy Consecration;

that, taking the Chalice which Thou dost offer to them, they
may say, "Not my will . . . not my will, but Thine . . .
O my God!"

that every morning, led on by them,

forming but one family in Thy Priesthood,
one single fold, under one single Shepherd,
together, we may mount Thine altar,
hungering and thirsting for Thee,
and resolved to make only one Victim, with the Victim,
for the salvation of the world;
in short, that they may be like the primitive Church . . .
that they may be our masters in sacrifice,
that they may be our leaders in love . . .

4.

Finally, all our brothers and sisters in Christ

who make profession of the Catholic and Apostolic faith;
all those who suffer in Germany, in Poland, in Austria . . . or
in hospitals . . . or in hovels . . . or in fine houses . . .
widows and orphans . . . the most obscure soul that
breathes in Asia, in Africa, in America . . . anywhere . . .
May my heart, O Christ, be like Thine . . . as wide as the
world!

And in our own country alone . . .

How many intentions!—
the great need of the seminaries to be filled, to be preserved,
to be developed in Thy love;
the great need of teaching vocations,
That instructors and instructresses be educated and schol-
arly, yes . . . but above all, directors of souls;
that our colleagues in the universities, freed from the re-
straint of their own home parishes, may be faithful to their
prayers;
that the masses of the working people, moved at last to
recognize in her, the Mother of the poor, may fall into the
arms of Thy Holy Church;

that the upper and lower middle classes may courageously
practice Holy Poverty . . . detachment from goods
tenaciously held on to . . . the divine improvidence of the
lilies and the little birds . . .
that our Catholic activities may escape becoming soulless business affairs, that their chaplains and promoters may come
forth from their Mass ready to cast fire on the world:
Ignem veni mittere in terram (Luc. XII, 49);
that husbands and wives may be truly the priests of their "great
Sacrament" and that they will form but one body, one
heart, and one soul, not for mere pleasure but to furnish
priests to the Church and elect to God!

*

*   *

For all these, for the most obscure, for the most forgotten, for
Our Holy Father the Pope, for our bishop and all bishops,
for our pastor and our curates and for all priests,
for all missionaries in distant lands, with all the fervor of
our souls, we bring Thee our offerings, *haec dona, haec
munera, haec sancta sacrificia.*
How this Canon, in the opening prayers, bids us practice the
"*quaerite primum regnum Dei* . . .
seek ye first the Kingdom of Heaven!"
We know that there is nothing else which matters: the grand
work of God! . . .
the Redemption of the world!
The Mass and the Canon, which is its essence, seem indeed like
the school of the grandeur of soul,
of the greatness of heart through the despoiling of it in silence
and adoration.
Ah, Lord, give to all Thy servants and handmaids
the grace to understand it a little better each day,
the grace to meditate each of its great prayers,
the grace to enter into it generously with all they possess,

and not to play truant, through an easy sentimental piety,
>   at the very moment when Thy Holy Church and Thou,
>   Thyself, O God, our Father,
wishest to give us the great and austere lessons
>   *OF THE SCHOOL OF LOVE.*

V

REMEMBER, LORD: PAUL,
YVONNE, LOUIS, LUCY . . .

Memento of the Living

But, dear Lord, we are allowed to make a remembrance of our
>   dear ones.
>   Originally, these precious names were unrolled at the Of-
>   fertory.
In order to bathe them in more intense prayer, our brethren of
>   the ages of faith asked that our loved ones might be re-
>   membered in the very heart of the Mystery, in the middle
>   of the Canon of the Mass.
And that is why now, after having prayed for all our brothers
>   and sisters of the entire Mystical Body, beginning with *our*
>   Pope and *our* Bishop,
it is Thy Will, O Heavenly Father, that we should recall to
>   Thee, by name, those whom we meet in our daily life,
>   at table, at home, at noon, and at night,
>   in our offices, our shops, our fields, and our places of busi-
>   ness . . .
those men and women who work with us, who suffer with us
>   . . . around us . . .
>   such a man . . . such a woman . . . among those whom
>   we know so well . . . among our relatives . . .
>   because they are sick or because . . . things are not going
>   well for them.

And then follow names . . .

       Paul . . . Yvonne . . . Lucy . . . Louis . . .

By their first names:
it is thus the priest mentions them in the Holy Sacrifice . . .
He calls them by their Christian name . . . that one which, in
    the home, we are inclined to turn into a pet name through
    a naive need of increasing our affection:
O Father, Thou the Father of the family, Thou callest Thy
    children thus . . . by their first name,
the name of our birth and of our burial, that which is marked
    with the seal of Thy Son, which is laden with the graces
    of Baptism.

    Peter, Mary, Madeline, Thy servants and handmaids . . .
no title, no rank, no distinction!
Even the Pope, even the Bishop, or the Marshal, or the King . . .
Before Thy Infinite Majesty, we are all . . .
    only Thy little servant . . . Peter or Maurice,
    only Thy little handmaid . . . Marie or Teresa.
All these words of the sacred text: brethren . . . servants . . .
    and handmaids, humble expressions in our worldly vocabu-
    lary,
    assume splendor and nobility in our Masses.
The individual . . . that is to say:
    the banker, the lawyer, the manufacturer, the weaver, the
    mason or the farmer, the ship owner or the cabin boy . . .
    in whatever rank he may be placed, in whatever work of
    life he may be,
    must be a *brother* . . . a *servant;* he must serve God and
    his brethren in Christ as a brother.
As soon as his pride stifles the *servant,*
as soon as his selfishness restrains the *brother,*
    there is no spirit of Christ in him.
Nay, worse . . . there is in him the Christianity of a worldling.

Lord, remember only Thy servants and handmaids: Paul,
Yvonne, Louis, Lucy.

Do not be too severe on their self-importance.

Remember their sufferings and their temptations and their
good will . . . and the dangers surrounding them.

At least they have not denied Thee, the Father, nor Thy Son,
nor the Holy Ghost.

Thou biddest us say that of the faithful who are dying
. . . why not of the faithful who are living?

Remember those who are present

with me . . . my dearly loved brethren of all classes . . . in
this church,

from the little child whom Thy Divine Son calls to Himself to caress and embrace . . . to the old man who is
standing near the confessional, turning his cap in his hands
while he is awaiting his turn for absolution.

Between these two, there is the little Jocist of the six o'clock
Mass who comes to bring Thee her whole heart and all the
actions of her day, for the salvation of her sisters.

There are the young Catholic actionists of the middle class who
have broken the bonds chaining them to their class and who
are now living as true Christians.

There are scouts and guides who understand the Mass and who
follow it in their Missals.

There is the manufacturer, the doctor, the broker, who have
discovered Christ and who come to seek Him and to carry
Him back with them to their offices.

There are the old men and old women, habitues of the seven or
eight o'clock Mass, each in his accustomed place—the
fourth one in the second pew, or behind the third pillar.

Lord . . .

their faith and devotion are known to Thee . . .

On all sides, more and more, great souls are discovering Thy
Son.
Thy Catholic Action bubbles and gushes forth from springs
—high and low and half-way up—
over all the declivities of the country.
Thy Spirit hovers over these subterranean waters which need
only to be gathered into forceful streams.
O God, our Father, remember sinners certainly, but remember
also these fervent souls, known or unknown to me . . .
here present or not . . . Grant that they be still more
fervent, more docile to Thy spirit, more empty of themselves.
Let them boldly burn the bridges behind them, and the little
passageways over which there still glide the considerations
of their self-love and their "respectability,"
and let them lose themselves entirely in Christ! . . .
Lord, grant that they may understand . . . and myself first of
all . . . that the sanctity of a single apostolic soul is one of
the major elements in the reconstruction of the world.

*For whom we offer, or who offer up
to Thee this Sacrifice . . .*

It is indeed for them that, all together—says the priest—*we offer
this Sacrifice.*
And to bring out more clearly our participation . . . as if
scrupulous about not having made it strong enough . . .
he stresses and asserts . . .
that we ourselves offer this sacrifice, *vel qui tibi offerunt
hoc sacrificium laudis.*
Lord, we heartily thank Thee for this grace of permitting us to
read in the sacred text our participation in Thy Sacrifice
and in Thy Priesthood,
our right to speak to Thee at this solemn moment, to tell

Thee our intentions in the Mass, and often our most intimate and most cherished secrets.
With what pride and what joy,

we offer Thee this sacrifice of praise.

We offer Thee, O Our Father, through the hands of the priest at the altar, this bread, this wine, which are to become the Flesh and the Blood of Thy Son Jesus Christ.
And through Him and in Him, we offer Thee also, at the same time . . . our flesh and our blood . . . our life, and particularly this present day in all its details . . .
for all the precious souls we have made remembrance of to Thee . . . for their salvation . . . for their sanctification . . . for the triumph of Catholic Action and of Thy Church,
in order that before Thee,

O God Eternal, living and true,

with Thy Son and His Holy Spirit, we may be in very truth, *the servants* that Thou desirest, brothers and sisters one to another,
those who are charged by Thee from all eternity to fill up what is wanting in the Passion of Thy Son.

VI

IN COMMUNION WITH AND HONORING
ESPECIALLY THE MEMORY OF THE
GLORIOUS EVER-VIRGIN MARY . . .

communicantes et memoriam venerantes . . .

O most sweet Virgin Mary, it is meet that thou shouldst be there at this moment of the Mass.

95

Thy Son Jesus will be among us soon . . .
and thou not be present?
He is the King, thou the Queen of the Church Triumphant.
Now the rendezvous around the Host is complete: the
angels, the saints, the souls in Purgatory and we . . . we
the church militant, thy children.
And . . . thou not be there?
O Mother, we are counting on thee . . .

. . . on thee first of all:

Imprimis gloriosae semper Virginis Mariae.
The liturgy is wise and true.
It gives thee thy place . . . the first.
It says: "in communion with, and honoring especially the memory of the glorious ever-Virgin Mary . . ."
It is then together, O Mother, that we participate in the Mass,
with thee at the head.
What joy to think that it is in union with thee . . .
that it is relying on thy prayer, on the fervor of thy
soul . . .
that we are going to offer Thy Divine Son to God all-
powerful.

And it is here that the assembling begins:

behind thee, the blessed Apostles, Peter and Paul, stand forth,
as likewise the others,
the first Popes of the age of the martyrs,
and the glorious martyr founders,
All that young primitive Church, without stain and without
wrinkle.
Thou givest them their places, as at a banquet, around the bread
and wine.
Art thou not she who presides?

The priest extends his hands over the chalice:

96

"We beseech Thee, O Lord . . ."

He says it in the plural. Thou sayest it with him and with us.

Thou beseechest the Father, the Son, and the Holy Spirit.

> And to thy supplication is joined that of thy noble company: the Apostles, the Popes, the Martyrs:
>
> all the grand sacerdotal family of the Church of yesterday and today have only one heart and one mind directed toward the Host.

We all beg for order, peace, eternal enrollment in the family of God.

> But especially . . .

ut nobis corpus et sanguis fiat . . .

"that the Body and Blood of Thy dearly beloved Son, Our Lord Jesus Christ, may be given to us. *Nobis . . . fiat.*

It is indeed for *us* that He comes . . . It is really *for us* that Thou callest Him, O most loving Mother.

With what assurance and what joy thou callest Thy Son and biddest Him come amongst us!

It is really through Thee that we possess Him at each Consecration.

> Each Mass is a grace which is a response to thy call.
>
> Each Host is a gift through thy prayer and almost from thy hand.

Qui pridie quam pateretur . . .

On the eve of His Passion,

> He was thinking of thee . . . thou wert not at table with the Apostles, but how near!
>
> In a neighboring room, perhaps . . .
>
> through a half-opened door or curtain, with Martha and Mary, perhaps Elizabeth, thou didst follow the scene.

Thou didst hear Him say: "This is My Body which will be delivered for you, this is my Blood . . ."

How these words must have struck against thy heart . . . This Flesh was His . . . and thine.

This Blood was His . . . and thine!

Thou didst hear Him say:

"Do this in commemoration of Me."

The Apostles were commanded to do it. And the bishops, successors of the Apostles, and the priests ordained by the bishops were bidden "to do this . . ."

that is to change bread and wine into the Body and Blood of thy Son.

How, O dearest Mother, could we fail to feel thee present in each of our Consecrations, in each of our Communions?

Thou art so bound to His Flesh and His Blood, to the Cenacle and the Cross.

The next day, in fact, when the tragic Reality succeeded the Figure,

thou wert there, standing, as on the preceding evening, delivering Thy Son to the executioners for the salvation of the world.

Who, in greater measure than thou, has offered the Host?

Who, in greater measure than thou, has been sacrificed with It?

Who, in greater measure than thou, has given his flesh and blood for the salvation of the world?

O heavenly Mediatrix,

receive, first of all, the gratitude and the love of thy children, of all those who so joyfully call thee "Mother."

All thy titles of glory, certainly, we love to give thee.

All thy diadems . . . for our pleasure and pride . . . we entreat thee

to place upon thy brow.

Nothing, we declare, nothing is too grand for our Mother, particularly the title of Mediatrix of all Grace.

But, can we give thee that of the Priesthood?

Some see thee at each Mass standing near the altar, as thou didst stand at the foot of the Cross . . .

Virgo Sacerdos . . . Virgin priest, holding in thy hands the Host.

We prefer, O most sweet Mother, to see thee among ourselves . . . in our pews, in the vanguard of those who have not received the Sacrament of Holy Orders,

but who are priests in so far as to participate in the Sacrifice and to offer, with the whole Church, the Body and the Blood of Thy Son.

Of those, thou art incomparably the first.

Mother of Christ, and our Mother, we see thee close to us . . . and close to Him.

We see thee indeed take our offerings from our hands and give them to Thy Son to weigh down the paten and the Host.

We see thee, as Mistress of the house, preparing the divine Table and giving us our places.

Thy glory and thy greatness, said Pius X, were not only to have furnished the Victim of Calvary, "the Body which He was to offer in Sacrifice and the Blood which He was to pour out for our redemption; thy mission was further to guard this Victim, to nourish It and to present It, on the appointed day, at the altar of Sacrifice."

Now, the Sacrifice continues.

Dost not thou also, O Mother, continue thy wonderful service?

Two immeasurable magnitudes among the masterpieces of God:

the *ordained priest* . . . the Priest for all eternity, of whom Christ makes use, to consecrate the Host,

and *Mary* . . . the Virgin Immaculate, Mother of God and

our Mother, Mediatrix between Christ and us for the pour-
ing forth of graces and the distribution of the Bread;
two magnitudes which are the Magnitude of God, but divided
up according to human measure.
In no one creature does God permit the combination.
But separated between two individuals, they can be asso-
ciated for Love.
And then opens the marvelous account of the great deeds of
Mary upon earth:
Mary takes her place at the head of all Christians to lead
them to the Host.
Thou art then present,
O Mother, at each of our Masses, at least in heart and mind.
In a few seconds, He will be there.
Thou knowest it since it is at thy prayer that He comes.
O Mother, so gentle and so sweet, take thy children, then, by
the hand to lead them to Him.
With us, we beg thee, bend over this table of stone on
which He will soon be born again and give us thy eyes to
contemplate Him,
thy prayer to adore Him,
thy heart to love Him
and to lose ourselves in Him.

VII

TO LOSE OURSELVES IN HIM

The Consecration

Hoc est enim Corpus meum—
Hic est enim Calix Sanguinis mei

This is the essential part of the Mass.

It takes two minutes . . . the time, O Lord, that it takes Thy
priest to say:

"This is My Body" . . .

"This chalice is the chalice of My Blood" . . .

And immediately Thou art on the altar, O adorable Master, in the verity of Thy Flesh and Blood . . . consecrated successively and separately to signify Thy mystic death in this Sacrifice.

Thou art present as Thou now art, glorious and resurrected, before the angels, the saints, and God . . .

perpetual Host of the Redemption which is being continued . . .

It is Thou, the only Priest,

Unique and ever-flowing fountain of our priesthood:

it is Thou Who, through the lips of the priest, ordained for this sublime function, dost pronounce these momentous Words . . .

and forthwith Thou continuest, Thou dost eternalize the solemn minute in which, rendering Thy last sigh . . .

Thou didst say: "All is consummated!" . . . It is finished. I have finished the task which was given me to do!

Ineffable instant . . .

in which the ransom of the world was an accomplished fact . . .

in which the Ocean of Infinity which separated sinful humanity from God was filled up.

Sublime minute of Silence, among all the minutes of history!

The only victory which merits to be endlessly continued . . .

to be endlessly recommenced . . . to be endlessly lived . . .

Lepanto, Austerlitz, the Marne . . . heroic instants, simply *commemorated*.

This victory of God over death and the sin of mankind . . .

this moment from the plenitude of God, in which the Father of the Prodigal Son receives back into His arms, hu-

manity and all creation, bathed and rejuvenated in the
Blood of His Son . . .
this moment of the satisfaction of God, in which nothing
of that which is not God misses the divine call . . .
this moment of the plenitude of Love and of Adoration,
and of Thanksgiving, and of conquering Expiation! . . .

Is an instant that never has an end.

Each Consecration gives *actuality* to it on earth . . . puts it
within our reach . . . at our very door.
It is like a gulf of Adoration, of Love and of Light . . . which
opens permanently under our eyes.
And I hear Thy Voice, O God, Thine ardent voice crying to
me: "Cast yourself in! Collaborate!"
Cast yourself in with the twelve months of this year which is
beginning . . . or which continues,
with all the joys, or troubles, or apprehensions which these
months conceal . . . with all the possible events, accidents
grave or trivial . . . with all the souls entrusted to you
and for whom you are responsible . . .
with all your thoughts, your words, your deeds,
with the slightest impulses of your mind and heart:
all that you previously cast into My Offertory is going to fall
into this torrent of My Adoration, of My Expiation, of My
Thanksgiving, and My Prayer . . .
And thus you cooperate in the joy of God . . . in the Love of
God . . . to His full satisfaction . . .
in His will to love the world and to complete its beauty
through the sanctification of souls.
Like a great fire, lighted in the middle of the world . . .
which gets closer and closer to the extremities of the earth,
devouring each blade of grass, each straw, and the harvests
and the forests, and the hamlets, and the cities . . .

and all that are numbered in the Church Suffering, Militant, and Triumphant,
thus, all is enflamed in Me . . . all becomes Love and holo-caust . . .
I am Myself the PRAYER of heaven and of earth, for the ran-som of worlds,
the sole Adoration living and glowing,
the sole Homage which transports all, in its rapturous ea-gerness . . . to the Feet of Infinite Majesty.

No one goes to My Father, except through Me.

Through Me, Christ of the Mass!
Through Me, the little consecrated Host!
Useless to try to pass to the right or left!
Useless to try to escape me!
You must enter in, with all your body . . . and all your soul . . . and all your days . . . weeks . . . months of this year . . .
with all the years of your life!
"Oh, how narrow is the way . . .
Oh, how low is the door which leads to Life!"
Thus speaks Christ. What can be said? What can be done?
It is the little way, the low door of the Host.
Here there can be no distinction, no exaltation of person!
Lower yourself! Diminish your importance . . . in order to pass!
You must bend low . . . you must immolate yourself . . .
you cannot collaborate without making yourself little . . .
as He does . . .
He alone is Lord here . . .
And see how tiny He is . . . The priest takes Him in his hands, and lifts Him toward God . . . and toward us.
See how He has reduced Himself to nothing, in order that His

103

Adoration and His Prayer may be pure and all-powerful before God.

Then, prostrate yourself! Make yourself one with the dust of the earth.

Make yourself one with Him in His humiliation!

And in the deep prostration of your body and your soul, with Saint Thomas, with all the saints, and the angels, and the whole universe,

and especially with Him, man like yourself,

so that your prayer may be His Prayer . . .

so that your adoration may be His Adoration,

so that your entire life may form a part of His Offering and His Sacrifice,

cry to this Host which soars above the universe:

"MY LORD AND MY GOD!"

VIII

WHEREFORE WE CALL TO MIND . . .

Unde et memores . . .

O Christ, Who art there on the corporal,
it is very sweet to obey Thee.

It is because Thou hast asked us to call to mind . . .
that we *do* call to mind . . .

we, Thy priests, ordained for this great Service,
and also we, simply baptised and confirmed, but because of this Baptism and this Confirmation, members of Thy great sacerdotal family.

In a tremendous silence of adoration and of love,
we call to mind . . .

we call to mind . . .

Thy blessed Passion, Thy precious Passion, the source of all grace and life for us.

How could we forget that at this moment?
    Thou art there on the altar,
    Thou Who wert the little Jesus of Bethlehem,
    Thou Who didst flee into Egypt when Thou wert not yet
    two months old . . .
    Thou Who, until the age of thirty, planed and sawed
    wood:
in all this, Thy Passion had already begun.

How could we forget

that first Consecration, in the Cenacle, into which Thou hadst
    already put Thy whole Heart,
    Thy whole Soul, all Thy Flesh and all Thy Blood,
    and that first Communion of Thy Apostles,
    and that first ordination of Thy priests,
    and the kiss of Judas,
    and Thine agony with the drops of Blood falling to the
    ground,
    and during that time, Thy best friends who were sleep-
    ing? . . .
How could we forget such excess of suffering which so forcibly
    showed Thy Love for us?
    and the blows, and the spittle, and the crown of thorns,
    and the nails in Thy Hands and in Thy Feet,
    and the lance of the centurion,
    and Thy Heart bleeding drop by drop to the very last . . .
    and finally Thy last sigh . . . that unforgettable minute
    that is being perpetuated?
    Thou art indeed He Who has suffered so much for us . . .
    and . . .
because Thou hast asked us to be appreciative and grateful
    and because it is an urgent need of our hearts,
    we call it to mind.
    We call to mind also Thy Resurrection and Thy glorious

because, for two thousand years, it has been the present, the
adorable Reality before our eyes.

It is easy to remember when we need only behold.

Yes! it is indeed the glorious Body of the Risen Lord Who is
there within our reach, under our hands, on the paten . . .
the Body of Him Who went up to heaven and returns
thence in all the veiled splendor of His Majesty.

The altar is truly a new Thabor,

but under the cloud . . .

With Peter, James, and John, with Moses and Elias, invisible around the Host,

we prostrate ourselves without seeing anything.

We know only through faith, that under the veil of the Host,

Thou art resplendent, O Christ, in adoration and in joy,
and that Thou dost inundate Heaven and earth with the
fire of Thy glory.

We know also . . . that . . .

this dim Thabor . . . is the Cross.

In this Sacrifice Thou hast united the glory of Thy Resurrection and Thy Ascension to the terrible moment of Thy
Passion . . . Was not one the condition of the other?

Was it not necessary that Thou shouldst suffer these things
and so enter into Thy Glory?

Thy past sufferings are present:

inexhaustible capital on which to draw for the salvation of
mankind,

ever real and permanent condition on which rests Thy
triumph and ours.

And thus it is that Thy Sacrifice . . . that of Golgotha . . . is
continued even here in this church . . . without tragic
horror . . . that is true . . . Thou canst no longer suffer
Thyself, O radiant Christ.

But Thou hast suffered, and we, Thy members, we can still
suffer,
and Thou dost rely upon us . . . is it not so? . . . to furnish this unbloody Sacrifice with sufferings, blood, thorns,
wounds,
though they be only those of our self-love,
though they be only drops of blood from our heart . . .
a modest fringe to Thy Host . . .
a tiny drop of water in Thy Blood.
    And behold all the sufferings of Thy Mystical Body . . .
flow together, at this moment, from the four quarters of the
world into this little chapel.
It seems that never have men suffered so much: Thy Passion is
being renewed again . . . and more.
Thy Passion . . . as of old, with the old tools of human
affliction: swords, whips, lances.
Thy members are hunted down, struck . . . as Thou wert,
for Justice and for Love.
Once more there are hasty flights in the middle of the
night.
There are also agonies of poor bodies tortured with pain in
clinics and hospitals.
There is the distress of souls embittered by their poverty, suffering from unemployment and from disgrace, shivering with
cold and hunger, in hovels, in fine houses, on the street . . .
Nay more, Christian countries ravaged, cut in two, where blood
flows from open veins on the field of fratricidal battle,
where the scourging is brought about by machine guns,
rifles, cannon, and bombs:
this is Thy Passion, O God, with the latest perfection of
science and of horror.
Ah! if Thou hadst not suffered so, we could not bear it.
But we are aware that in the same proportion
Thou makest Thyself in Thy Sacrifice, loving and importunate.

How confidently we feel that Thy glory and Thy joy are meant only to absorb all our woes, our sadness, our agonies . . .
to console them, to cure, to compassionate them, to drown them in Thy Splendor . . .
to make them strong in the fight for the salvation of others: to give them the glory of being Thy associates in the Redemption of the world,
and the nobility: that Thy Sacrifice may be truly theirs.
O Christ, grant that we may rise to that!
Give this grace to those whom Thou no longer callest Thy disciples, but Thy friends, Thy brothers and sisters.
And permit them now to say to Thy Heavenly Father with deep gratitude,
with a noble pride which pierces through the tears of their confusion . . .
the marvelous liturgical words of the oblation, complete and definitive:

We offer up to Thy Excellent Majesty . . .

De tuis donis ac datis. The ineffable Gift which Thou hast willed us to make:
"the pure Host, the holy Host, the immaculate Host":
Thy Divine Son Himself:
"the Sacred Bread of life
and the chalice of our eternal Salvation":
We offer it to Thee, O Father, with the whole Church, in virtue of that part of the priesthood conferred on us in Baptism;
with Him, in Him, through Him,
we offer Thee all the sufferings of our poor humanity throughout all the whole world:
we offer Thee especially our body, our soul, our blood, our life.

108

O adorable Trinity, in Thine august Presence, under Thy silent
watchfulness:
it is the same magnificent and burning Host!

How could we hope to

offer Thee, by ourselves, a like sacrifice?
How could we have dreamed of presenting ourselves before
Thee with the expectation of being considered?
But see, now, our petty sufferings and our weak sighs receive
attention and plead even irresistibly in our behalf.
Behold our wretched prayer, united with that of Thy Son,
shakes the gates of Heaven.
Behold us . . . helpless sinners that we are . . . as soon as the
contact is made with our Christ, as soon as we touch but
the hem of His garment, we are empowered to present
ourselves at Thy Throne, confidently and fearlessly, as-
sured of a loving welcome.
Why?

Christ is there, on the altar . . .

enveloping us with His Light, incorporating us in His Flesh, in
His Blood, in His Soul, in His Life . . . saying to His Fa-
ther what He said to His Apostles:
"O My Father . . .
"What you do to the least of these, you do to Me."
O dearly beloved Christ, we wish *to call to mind* all Thy words.

IX

THE RESURRECTION WITH CHRIST
IN THE HOLY SACRIFICE

Permit, Lord, that we return to the edge of this grand Mystery of Thy Holy Consecration, and even, aided by the

light of Thy Holy Spirit, that we may try to descend
further into its abysses.

Grant us especially the grace of a new fervor, and that each
Mass may be for us a *resurrection*.

If the Mass is the continuation of the Passion,
is it not also like an Easter morning when a few precious
friends . . . ourselves among them . . . a few holy
women come running at dawn?

And now the priest inclines

profoundly. The rubrics demand it of him.

It is with intense recollection that he pronounces words, which
are more than a prayer, which are a mystical and ardent
supplication:

"We humbly beseech Thee, . Almighty God, command these
offerings to be carried by the hands of Thy holy Angel to
Thine Altar on high, in the presence of Thy Divine Majesty . . ."

Why, Lord, from Thy priest and from us, such a demonstration
of respect . . . almost prostration?

Why incline so profoundly? why supplicate Thee so forcefully?

Has something new come to pass, unnoticed?

Have we not just completed a prayer, sufficient and full?

The offering of the pure, holy, immaculate Host to Thy Most
Excellent Majesty . . . *Offerimus praeclarae Majestati
tuae* . . . is it not the final prayer *par excellence*, beyond
which there is no other prayer?

We beseech Thee . . .

Supplices te rogamus. O God, Our Father, with all the force
that our poverty gives us . . . with our whole being
stretched out in its misery and its impotence . . .

we beseech Thee, fill up what is yet wanting.

Thou hast inspired us with this strengthening joy, to offer ourselves, to cast ourselves body and soul into the fire of the
Consecration of Thy Son . . .
but there is something more satiating, more intoxicat-
ing . . .
It is not much to be at the door, with hands full, and to knock
. . . to knock . . .
What is more affecting is to be with arms outstretched, the door
opened.
And even with arms outstretched . . . it is little or nothing! . . .
There is something far more eager, far more affecting than
outstretched arms . . .
There are the actual outpourings of love . . .
There is the Father who receives His Son on His heart and
communicates to Him all the secrets of His love and of His
life.
In a word, Lord . . . always the same anxiety of Thy chil-
dren . . .
They are not satisfied with offering themselves.
They want to be accepted, they want to be able to plunge
themselves into Thee . . . They long to fall into Thy
Arms!

They must become one with Thee . . .

Jube haec perferri . . .
We beseech Thee, grant us this supreme joy
of becoming one with Thee,
with all that we have placed on the altar beside the Host
. . . our thoughts, our heart, our flesh, our life.
Thy Son, O Holy Father, Thou wilt always receive.
Thou hast never refused His offering.
His sacrifice is altogether agreeable. It is consummated. It
is perfect.

111

But we? . . . Art Thou going to leave us along the way, weary
and sorrowing?

After having inspired us with an immense hope and having carried us to this meeting with Thee, having conducted us almost to the threshold of Love . . .

to this divine union which is Thy Sanctity . . .

art Thou going to treat us like foolish virgins?

Lord, if our heart lacks this oil of radiant and sensible devotion,

nevertheless, I assure Thee, with this little dry heart, we
desire eagerly to love Thee.

Our lamp is not extinguished . . . See. There still remains a
little smoke.

Then, remember that Thy Son said in our regard:

"Do not quench the smoking flax."

And that is why every morning we run to Him, our risen Christ,
to be caught, rekindled, and carried to Thee by Him.

O Father, Thou wilt not deceive Thy children.

"*Jube haec perferri* . . . Grant that we may be received
by Thee."

By the hands of Thy holy angel.

Per manus sancti angeli tui . . .

For that purpose, O Lord, Thou hast angels at Thy disposition.

Certainly, Thou dost not lack assistance. Companies, legions, of
angels are ready to fly at Thy slightest signal,

perhaps, above all, the Angels of Prayer and of Sacrifice, or that
Angel whom Saint John saw standing before the altar with
the golden censer.

Whether they be one or many, whom Thou designest for this
office, they must be subject to the orders of Thy Son.

All that they take from our daily life:

our slightest thoughts . . . our most trivial words . . .
our tiniest deeds . . .

on the street, at work . . . while visiting . . .
everything that lives and breathes . . . everything joyful,
everything sorrowful . . .
yes, all that, let Thy holy angels gather.
Let them fill our Offertory baskets! . . .
And may Thy Divine Son, the Master of Angels, the Angel of
the Great Council . . . the Holy Angel *par excellence,*
take hold of the modest gifts of Thy baptised children with
His Redeeming Hands, and add them to the Host,
that there may be only one single glorified Host, divinized,
one single Sacrifice on earth as in Heaven, to the glory of
Thy Divine Majesty . . .

To Thine altar on high

In sublime altare . . .
Is such an elevation possible for Thy little creatures?
this resurrection to a supernatural life?
this incredible good fortune?
To be received by Thee, O God our Father!
to be laid with Thy Son and by Him, on Thine *altar on
high:*
the least among us . . .
and even, by preference, the least, and the greatest also if
they become little . . .
all, with their most insignificant actions . . .
a sweeper with her broom, a seamstress with her needle and
scissors,
a stenographer with her notebook and pencil,
a housekeeper with her market bag . . .
all suddenly glorified . . . all brought out of insignificance and,
as from the dust of the tomb, received by Thee as forming
part of the Sacrifice,
and finally, placed in the scale with ages and peoples in the
solemn and final negotiations in the ransoming of souls.

In the presence of Thy Divine Majesty.

. . . In conspectu divinae majestatis . . .

It takes place before Thee . . . or rather in Thee, O God our
Father,
    in Thy paternal bosom where from all eternity, within
    Thy Son, we have lived together.
And now, Thou still wishest us to be together and Thou makest
    no distinction between Thine only-begotten Son and Thine
    adopted children.
With Hands full, Thy Son takes hold of us
    and offers us to Thy Majesty and places us once more with
    Himself in Thy paternal bosom
    where we shall live together forever
    because henceforth we form one single Host.
That Host, submerged in Thee,
    Thou art going to restore to us all flowing with graces,
    still warm and palpitating with Thy Life eternal.
Oh! that marvelous going-out and coming-back of Christ Who
bears us with Him, and Who returns to the point of His
departure to bury us still deeper in Love.
Oh! that ceaseless Way in the journey towards Infinity we make
    in Him!
Oh! that perfect Gift which together we make to God for the
    plenitude of His glory, and which comes back to us for our
    glorious immortality . . .
    in order that all those who shall have communicated . . .
with the priest during this Mass . . .
    ut quotquot ex hac altaris participatione . . .
    who shall have participated in this Sacrifice . . .
first by delivering themselves up body and soul to the Host
    . . . victims with the Victim . . . then afterwards, by re-
    ceiving this same Host all irradiated with divine glory,
and receiving in It and with It, the Sacrifice Itself,
    and the Divine Sacrificer with all His splendor, with all

114

His power of Expiation, of Imploration, of Justification, of
Glorification . . .
in order that all present . . . all these participating in Thy
priesthood, O Christ, and in thy Sacrifice
. . . may be filled with all heavenly benediction and grace . . .
omni benedictione coelesti et gratia repleamur.
If we really want to rise gloriously from here below,
we must first offer ourselves with the Victim;
we must pass through the narrow way of the Host;
we must reduce ourselves to the point of utter renunciation.
It is through contact with the *Victim Christ* that we do what
is necessary to be spiritualized.
But it is through our union with *Christ glorious* . . .
through this Communion with the Christ Who returns
straight from the bosom of the Father, rich with glory,
with warmth, and with life,
that we are vivified, glorified, and blessed.
A benediction which is not of the earth:
all the benedictions of Heaven . . .
the most beautiful gifts that one can carry back from a
glorious voyage to the country of Light, of Beauty, and
of Infinite Love:
a fullness of soul—*repleamur*—
a spiritual satisfaction,
an unalterable serenity which passes all human compre-
hension . . .
a resurrection so high and so complete
that everything that is not of this new life exhales an odor
of death . . .
His life in us, His thoughts, His devotedness, His Sacrifice at
every hour of the day and night, His poverty, His self-de-
nial for the saving of souls, His Holy Spirit Itself . . .
all that is not possible, O Christ, unless, immolated with Thee,

Thou causest us to pass with Thee into the bosom of the
Father,
unless Thou dost nourish Thy little creatures with Thy pure
and glorious Flesh,
primary resurrection in advance of the other, certain pledge
of our immortality.
O Christ, *Jube haec perferri,*
in the transport of Thy Heart that loves us so much, bear
us up with Thee!

X

REMEMBER ALSO, LORD, PETER . . .
JAMES . . . MARY . . . ELIZABETH . . .
MEMENTO OF THE DEAD

Remember also . . .

O God, Our Father,
in the presence of the Host, because of Thy Divine Son Who
has been sacrificed . . . remember Thy servants and hand-
maids who have gone before us with the sign of faith.
But how couldst Thou forget them, since for Thee to remember
is to see?
Ceaselessly Thou seest them without, alas, their seeing
Thee!
O Our Father, do not rest content with *seeing* them.
Look upon them! . . . Be mindful of them!
We who no longer see them at all,
we who see only the place left empty . . .

we remember so well! . . .

Perhaps, too well . . . we are reminded of them . . .
Here is the footstool . . . the table . . . the desk . . .
where, a few days ago . . . a few months, even a few

116

years . . . after all, the years are only months and days . . .

they were seated (father, mother, wife, husband, brothers, sisters, children, grandchildren). For, dear Lord, Thou sendest Thy call at every age.

Here are their rooms respected . . . venerated almost like chapels . . . untouched as if yesterday they went away, on a voyage; as if they would return this evening or tomorrow.

Here are their books . . . their little trinkets . . .

and the great portraits in the drawing-room

and the little pictures on the mantelpiece, around the clock;

and the albums on the table bulging with vacation snapshots.

Here are their graves, well cared for, decorated with flowers, often visited . . . a real pilgrimage!

Oh! how mindful we are of them!

Be Thou also mindful . . . let us together be mindful of those we love.

Peter . . . James . . . Mary . . . Elizabeth . .

Thus, we know, the Church speaks.

Now, if while living, the Church recognizes us by our given name, how much more reason in death . . .

Alas! . . . We are not satisfied. We struggle furiously against the effacements of Death.

Having no longer the person, we want at least

to preserve the "personality" with his name:

the name on his visiting card, and on his door plate, and in the telephone book,

the name of the marriage contract and of wills,

the name so familiar to lawyers, bankers, and tax collectors,

the name perhaps still resplendent with nobility and proved integrity . . .

but which in the course of years, far from its Pure Source,
became a bit tarnished with pride, frivolity, and sin,
Lord, Thou canst be heard in Death!
Do remember Peter . . . James . . . Mary . . . Elizabeth . . .

Thy servants and handmaids . . . thy service

—their sole employment! their only profession! . . . to whom
Thou didst say, "Come!"
and who came immediately, like good servants,
to take their places in the interminable line . . .
and who form our advance-guard on those vast unknown roads
of Thine eternity . . .
where we shall soon join them again . . .
with so many . . . so many others . . . all those who are dying this minute, eighty-seven . . . eighty-eight, about a
hundred a minute, 140,000 today,
fifty-one million this year, who will pass, O Lord, to Thy cross-
roads . . . and who will be taken between crossfire, like
an army in rout . . . the fire of hell . . . and that . . . of
Purgatory.
O Master! what poignant mystery is that of Thine elections and
Thy rejections!
How many of these souls have passed the Examination on
Love?
Crushed and prostrate before Thine Infinite Majesty, we can
only say to Thee:
"Remember . . . Remember my dear ones and all those
. . . those who are mine and above all . . . Thine . . ."
Cast one look upon them in their distress,
in their great solitude, in their immense poverty, in their
hunger and thirst for Thee,

118

in this fire which Thou hast created for their purification
to make shine on their brow like a pure diamond:

the sign of Faith:

the only jewel which they carry into eternity . . .
the sole title by which they will salute us in the Mansion of
God . . .
this seal of Thy Son . . . this stamp of Jesus Christ . . .
this indelible decoration . . . the only one which forms part of
the soul,
sigillum, divine seal which is nothing else than participation in the priesthood of Thy Son . . .
by which they are Thy children, Thy soldiers, and Thy
priests . . .
by which they had that power, when they were still with
us,
of taking, through the hands of Thine ordained priest, the
consecrated Host, and of offering It to Thee for their salvation and that of the whole world . . .
Perhaps they did not do it when they could.
Now they are no longer able. We must do it for them, as for
infants and for the aged . . .
as for those in captivity . . .
as for those who sleep a heavy sleep.
O God, Our Father, permit that in their name, through the
hands of the priest at the altar, I may take the Host to offer
It to Thee in expiation for their weakness and their faults.

"For all those souls dear to me . . ."

mine and Thine . . . O Our Father, for all those who rest in
Christ . . .
those who died today, yesterday, and through the ages . . .
for the most forgotten, the poorest, the most abandoned
. . . I pray . . . or rather . . .

it is not I who pray . . . it is He, He Whom I have at my disposal, Thy Christ immolated . . .

He Who wearied Himself pursuing them here below . . . He Who has given for them His Blood to the last drop.

It is His Blood which cries to Thee, stronger than the blood of Abel, than the blood of all Thy martyrs, than the blood of my poor heart.

O Father, with this Host at hand, permit Thy children to be bold even to indiscretion.

Grant that quickly . . . they may attain those high places of Refreshment, Light, and Peace, *locum refrigerii lucis et pacis* . . .

where Thou hast prepared the sublime altar of Thy Divine Majesty.

Grant that having in one hand the Ransom of the whole world, they may with the other knock at Thy Door.

O Father, art Thou not our Accomplice?

Hast Thou not given us Thy Son, that we may make use of Him?

"The Mouth of Jesus Christ on the cross is become our mouth, and through It we speak to the Father to appease His Anger; His Heart which has been transpierced has become our heart and through it, we love the Father" (Saint Augustine).

Forming only one with Him, with His invincible Force, could we not at least push the gate of Heaven, and open it a little, in order that from Thy Gardens there may come, in little gusts, some refreshment, and some symphonies which may be an alleviation to these poor souls and something of a prelibation of joy before the eternal inebriation?

And even, pushing our boldness to the limit . . .

having in hand the Means of saving mankind, could we not ask Thee to deliver at least a few souls?

Behind those radiant gates, partly opened, art Thou not standing, O Our Father, with arms outstretched to watch for them, to welcome them, to ravish them with Thy Beauty and to plunge them into Thyself?

O Abyss . . . O inexhaustible Source of Refreshment, Light, and Peace! . . .

Have mercy . . . please ! . . .

. . . *Ut indulgeas deprecamur* . . .

Such are our humble and demanding claims.

But hast Thou not already loosed some bonds?

Has not the pleading of the Blood of Thy Son made the fire recoil?

Mystery! No angel, even that of the Sacrifice, will come to tell us the number of rapt souls who will be transported to heaven this day, and . . .

what is the balance between those coming in and those going out . . .

Deprecamur. Our rôle is to pray . . . to supplicate with the great Mendicant Who ceaselessly intercedes with the Father . . . with our Christ . . .

We can do no better than to forget ourselves . . . to lose ourselves in Him . . . to let ourselves be swept along by His holy desire for souls, and to draw from His Heart, for our poor exiles and for ourselves . . .

hunger and thirst for God.

And thus, devotion to the holy souls in Purgatory becomes devotion to the Beatific Vision.

To desire God for them . . . to desire God for ourselves passionately!

To desire passionately Infinite Purity, Holiness, Love, in the vision of God.

O Lord, in the name of these famished souls,

for the honor of Sovereign Reality,

grant that finally we may be dissatisfied with appearances and images and approaches . . .

O Thou, Whose great Shadow passes and repasses behind the screen of this world, when shalt Thou cease to be a reflection?

When shalt Thou finally come before our eyes, quite clearly: The Light?

O holy souls who are still thirsting, we share with you this torment . . .

Give us a little of your Purgatory!

Give us your hunger and thirst for God!

And you, the satiated . . . you the inebriated . . .

you especially, who have been delivered during this past minute . . .

you, the brilliant prize of our ever-efficacious sacrifice,

sing . . . sing with the Angels and the Principalities . . . and the Dominations . . . and the Virtues . . . the *Sanctus* . . . *Sanctus* . . . *Sanctus* face to face with God!

Exult in the Refreshment and in the Light . . . But . . .

think also of those millions of souls whom you have left in prison . . .

think of your loved ones groaning . . . think of those holy souls ever longing and ever being held off . . .

and think of us also, of the Church Militant, in this land of exile which is the initial Purgatory.

Through the Sacrifice of Christ, we have just opened for you the gates of Heaven.

This Sacrifice which has delivered you, we began here on earth without you.

Now, without us, make it complete in Heaven.

Offer to the Infinite Majesty, for our salvation and sanctification, the eternal Host which you now possess.

O beloved souls, satiated with love, do not forget . . .

that though you can no longer hunger and thirst for
God . . .
With God Himself, you can hunger and thirst for us.

XI

A LITTLE PLACE, LORD,
AMONG YOUR GREAT MARTYRS . . .
NOBIS QUOQUE PECCATORIBUS

To us sinners also . . .

who trust in Thy mercy, Lord . . . for Thou hast already been
so merciful . . .
deign to grant an alms also to us poor beggars, who are stretching out our arms to Thee.

Some part and fellowship.

Give us a little part . . . Give us a place . . . the last . . .
in that admirable company of Thy martyrs who mount
guard around the Host . . . And what a guard! . . .
The Church has invited thither her proudest knights . . . a
sort of Legion of Honor of martyrs . . .

Saint John the Baptist

Prophet of the Most High . . . foremost, powerful of soul,
electrifying young people and gathering them around him.
But as soon as he saw Thee, O Christ . . .
Ah! what disinterestedness! . . . he pointed Thee out to his
young disciples:
"It is to Him," he said, "that you must go . . .
"I am only the voice that goes before. Behold the Lamb of
God! I am not worthy to loose the latchet of His shoes. He
must increase and I must decrease!"
Thy Truth only was of consequence to him. He was not afraid
to say to one of the great ones of this world: *"Non licet*

. . . You have no right to keep the wife of your brother."
And he paid for this candor with his head.

Lord, *partem aliquam et societatem* . . . Give Thy children
here on earth a little of this loyalty . . . a little of this
courage.

Saint Stephen . . .

the first of the martyrs of the New Testament,
"full of grace and of strength" . . . his soul full of the Holy
Spirit . . . His adversaries could not resist the Wisdom and
the Spirit that spoke through his mouth . . . Then, grind-
ing their teeth and withered away with envy and anger,
seeing lightning flashing on his forehead,
they cast stones at this brilliant target . . . but the stones of the
torrent were sweet to him . . . (and seeing Thee, he said):
"Lord, here is my soul, but lay not this sin to their charge!"
O Lord! Give us a little of this greatness of soul . . . Thine
own . . . which pardons enemies . . .
and let the insults . . . let the stones which we receive be sweet
to us also, that it may be a proof that we love Thee.

Saint Matthias and Saint Barnabas:

Saint Matthias . . . who replaced Judas . . . repaired . . .
counterbalanced the sin of Judas! . . .
What an abyss to fill!
Moreover, he did the work of two, three, four, ten!
Lord, it may well be said of us, that we have work to do for
two, for three, for four, for ten . . . for a whole village
even, and for a whole city.
Therefore, Lord, *aliquam partem* . . . Give us Saint Matthias
as our trainer! . . . And Saint Barnabas . . . the great
friend of Saint Paul . . . The two friends, after having
missioned together, separated because . . . they could not
agree! Is it possible?

Yes! Lord, we know it is possible and that it actually happened . . .

It did not prevent their agreeing to give Thee all their time, all their strength, and all their blood . . .

Ah! Lord, again, *partem aliquam.*

Grant that in spite of disputes and complications, we may agree in substituting for one another and in loving Thee unto death.

Saint Ignatius, bishop of Antioch:

No one showed more fearlessness, more enthusiasm for martyrdom: loaded with chains for the love of Jesus Christ, he wrote to the Christians of Rome:

"I fear your charity. I fear that you have a too human affection for me. You could perhaps keep me from dying . . . there is no more beautiful work for you to do than to let me die . . . Suffer me to be immolated while the altar is ready . . . Being a Christian does not consist in fine words . . . it is greatness of soul, it is solidity of virtue . . . If ever, under trial, through weakness, I let escape other sentiments, do not believe . . . Let me become the prey of lions and bears. I am the wheat of God. I must be ground under their teeth in order to become a bread worthy of Jesus Christ." (Letter of Saint Ignatius, written at Smyrna and entrusted to the Christians going to Rome, 107–116 A. D.)

Lord! Again *partem aliquam* . . .

Not so much fine words as fearlessness!

Not so much fine songs as the spirit to go to meet the difficulties, perhaps the persecutions which await us!

Alexander, Marcellinus, and Peter:

Alexander, a young Pope thirty years old . . . the Pope of the drop of water added to the wine in the chalice. It is he who prescribed this rite in the Mass . . .

125

But he was the valiant Christian of the Roman nobility . . .

> "He completely converted it, including the Prefect of
> Rome. And for this good deed, the Emperor Hadrian or-
> dered his body to be transfixed with swords." (May 3,
> 117.) Evidently this was the price!

Peter, simple exorcist, also a strong defender:

"Having been imprisoned, he converted Pauline, the
daughter of his jailor, then her father and mother . . . then all
the family and household. Hearing of this, the Judge Serenus,
angered by this series of conversions, ordered that their necks
be cut after they had been made to lie on broken glass!" (304)
It was the price also.

Oh! Lord! What a mystery! What indefatigable passion for
> gaining souls . . .

Saint Perpetua and Saint Felicitas:

Here we are at the height of gallant conduct!

Saint Felicitas, pregnant for eight months . . . a slave!

Perpetua, of noble family, mother of a child she was nursing!

Felicitas feared that she would not be ready for the "Day of
> Spectacles."

"Then, in prison, all the brethren (the Christians) prayed
to obtain her deliverance. Three days later, a jailor who heard
her groaning as she was giving birth to her child, said, 'If you
complain now, what will you do before the beasts?' 'Now,' she
answered, 'it is I who suffer; but in the circus, Christ will suffer
for me, because I shall suffer for Him.'" Perpetua, on her part,
withstood the assaults of her father and kinsfolk: "My daughter,
have pity on your father. Have pity on your child. Sacrifice for
the welfare of the emperors!" "I will not do it, I cannot do it,
for I am a Christian."

And Perpetua, the patrician, and the slave, Felicitas, went to the
> amphitheater hand in hand, smiling and festively arrayed;

for in order not to appear sad going to martyrdom, through
a sublime coquetry, they were attired as for a ball.

O delicacy! O greatness of soul!

Lord! . . . *Nobis quoque peccatoribus!* . . . We can say no
more . . .

And so for Agatha, Lucy, Cecilia, Agnes, Anastasia:

Young virgins, young women cut down in the flower of their
youth . . . frail and vibrant, snatched from their drawing-
rooms to be dragged into infamous places and . . . passing
through like a pure flame, inviolate . . .

coping with judges, governors, prefects, a whole circus unchained,

offering the world this unheard-of spectacle: patricians and
slaves, when about to die, embracing one another as sisters,
and together, in unbelievable ecstasy, giving their blood as
a burning witness of their Baptism and of their union with
Christ.

Christianity of old be for us of today! . . .

From the purest heights of Thy Church, Lord, descends this
great breath of refreshment, enthusiasm, and of love . . .
Oh! let it be our strength!

Poor weak Christians of today, around Thine altar,
together, we have just cast into Thy Consecration our souls
and our lives.
Will it be but a splendid gesture?

What shall we do before the public mocker in the shops, in the
offices, in the dockyards, in the market places, and on the
street?

Lord, in order that we may stimulate others, inspire us with the
spirit of Thy martyrs!

Give us a place among the great soldiers of Thy Guard.

Certainly not because of our merits,

Non aestimator meriti . . .
>   we are too miserable for that splendid company.

But, since Thy church, dear Lord, invites us . . .

in Thine indulgence, O Thou the Director of Martyrs, permit
>   us at least to bathe ourselves in this ardor of Thy young
>   Church, so that we may come forth firmly resolved that
>   when we offer ourselves at the Offertory of the Mass . . .

it is with the intention of being truly immolated at the Consecration!

XII

O Christ, Sublime Engineer of Heaven and Earth

PER QUEM HAEC OMNIA

>   *Haec omnia* . . . all these things

the bread, the wine . . .

and all those things which, at one time, the people used to bring
>   to the Offertory: the first fruits:
>   corn, grapes, fruits, vegetables, oil, wax, and honey—

all these things were placed on the altar around the Host, to
>   receive the benediction of Christ and of the priest . . .

Christ presiding at this creation in miniature,

Christ among His own, creature Himself in the midst of crea-
>   tures, making Himself according to His custom the least
>   of all.

>   O Christ, the least of all and the first of all,

it has not been Thy Will to eclipse with Thy Splendor the
>   blade of grass and the grain of sand . . .
>   A simple bunch of grapes . . .
>   how sumptuous it appears! . . .
>   A full ear of corn! . . .
>   how glorious . . .

And Thou art unequaled beauty in Thy whiteness amongst the
honey and wax of Thy bees,
the grape of Thy vines . . .
and the corn of Thy harvests . . .
Simple little piece of Bread!
the first . . . because it is the last . . .

At this same moment, O Christ,

Thou art directing the stars and the oceans, sublime Engineer
of all the wonderful networks of heaven and earth,
and silently Thou callest to this rendezvous of highest
worship
the most glorious, the most sparkling of Thy stars, that they
may form the brilliant setting for our humble and mute
offerings,
that tied all together in Thy Hand, they may be the glittering
bouquet of creation, presented to the Father by Thee.
All the glory of heaven and earth remain under
the veil with Thee.
O Thou, Who art Love at the same time as Thou art Bread,
O Thou, Who art irreproachable Justice and pure Holiness
. . . and Prayer and inebriating Beauty . . . at the same
time as Thou art Bread,
Thou chargest Thyself with vivifying, sanctifying . . .
blessing all our gifts
that they may be made acceptable
to Infinite Majesty.
The supreme excellence of these ears of corn, of these grapes,
is in being presided over by a Host,
is in being presented by Thee,
Our Christ!

We no longer enjoy

those long impressive Offertory processions, when the whole

129

congregation formed in line . . . carrying the gifts which
Thy bounty allowed them . . .

Now the offering is made under the lowly obscurity of symbol.
O Christ, *Thou* bringest Thy great constellations and Thy
stars, and Thy mountains, and Thine oceans . . .

Nothing is to be seen, yet everything is there.

We, too, bring to Thee invisibly the offering of our day . . .
all we do, whether with spades, rakes, hammers, machines,
autos, boats, books, registers . . .

Nothing is to be seen, yet everything is there.

Invisible and glorious,

Come to us, O Christ, as Thou art.

Be indeed our Bread in order to be our Justice and our Beauty
and our Prayer and our Love and our Glory,
in our most trivial actions.

Make us hunger and thirst for Thee,
in order that we Christians of today may be indeed the
companions—if not of the noble martyrs of the *Nobis
quoque peccatoribus*, at least of those who formed in line
at the Offertory, eagerly bringing

their wheat, their grapes, their wax, and their honey . . . and
their love . . . and all the blood of their hearts.

XIII

TO THE MASTER OF HEAVEN AND EARTH BE ALL HONOR AND GLORY

(Recapitulation in Christ)

PER IPSUM ET CUM IPSO ET IN IPSO . . . OMNIS HONOR ET GLORIA . . .

Taking in his hands the Sacred Host,
the priest holds it over the Precious Blood in order to unite

130

them, and he proclaims that:

per Ipsum . . . through Jesus

cum Ipso . . . with Him

in Ipso . . . in Him,

are rendered to the Father Almighty, in union with the Holy Spirit,

all honor and glory.

Then . . . we have the slight action of the little Elevation.

This rite, one of the most important of the Sacrifice, is barely noticed now . . .

A light tinkling of the little bell warns the most attentive of the faithful . . . up to the eleventh century, it was the one solemn Elevation.

From the *Te igitur*, all the priests who concelebrated with the bishop . . . remained inclined.

During the Canon, the whole congregation observed total silence.

And when the celebrant reached the *Per Ipsum*,

elevating Host and Chalice,

bells or trumpets were sounded.

Inclinations were made more profound.

The entire congregation was bowed in adoration.

For a momentous action was taking place,

the most sublime of the Mystery of Faith,

its very Reason and Essence:

the gathering together of all created things and their ascent to the very throne of God.

O Lord, permit Thy lowly creature to retrace with Thee the stages of this wondrous journey.

The Offertory of man! . . .

First offertory! . . .

despoiling oneself of all earthly things . . .

131

the gathering together of all creation and of people living and
dead . . .
as well as the tiniest fraction of our lives.
We bring ourselves, soul and body . . .
we bring the universe . . . we bring everything to Thy
altar, Lord,
so that this little chapel, or this village or city church, or this
vast cathedral would be ridiculously small . . .
if it were not for our hearts . . . our human heart which Thou
hast made immense.
Oh! our vocation demands that we
enlarge our hearts to the dimensions of heaven and earth!
and to sing with a loud voice:
Pleni sunt coeli et terra gloria tua.
Lord, we thank Thee humbly for having made man, priest and
summit of Thy creation . . . and for having willed . . .
that, through our hands, each grain of human dust should take
the way of return.
But . . . what a disappointing task . . .
What zigzags . . . how many times must we spring back
to advance a few steps!
And then, in the last analysis, whatever may be our spirited
hopes and our unchained energy, there are insurmountable
boundaries.
Before that final bar, that frail barrier which cuts the horizon . . .
we have to stop . . . Impossible!
absolutely impossible to pass beyond!
Man's efforts would be in vain:
he can never be more than man.
Eternal pilgrims of Emmaus on that way of return to God—
we could with good reason despair . . . if . . . some mys-
terious Voyager did not join us suddenly on the way.

                              The Offertory of the Church,

Thou art here, O Christ!

At every instant, Thou risest up on our altars, *Hoc est enim corpus meum*, each time the priest says that.

And immediately the Church, thy Spouse, recognizes her Well-beloved.

She salutes Thee, she adores Thee . . . It is the first Elevation.

And she offers Thee to God our Father:

Offerimus praeclarae Majestati tuae . . . de tuis donis ac datis . . .

Of all these good things there on the altar, she chooses the Good *par excellence*, the ineffable Gift:

Hostiam puram, Hostiam sanctam, Hostiam immaculatam . . .

the one which includes them all: *omnia in Ipso constant.*

Everything that has been created . . . all the grains of dust gathered together from this earth . . . including myself . . .

all that part of creation lost in space,

which has already found its way back . . .

and which comes to an end in us: . . . Man . . .

Lo! it now receives from Thee, O Christ, a marvelous increase, its summit, its spiritual plenitude, and likewise a purity, a sanctity . . . the pure whiteness of sacrifice.

Now, this offering of the entire world

the Church may offer to the Father, offering Thee Thyself.

But that is all . . . She can only offer . . .

She can only stretch forth her arms . . . without reaching the goal.

Led on by the folly of the saints, she may

dream, like Saint Teresa of Avila,

of proceeding alone with her precious burden

to the meeting with Infinity.

With a little faith, like a grain of mustard seed, she may lift
some little mountain some few inches.
All the same, she could not raise all the mountains at once and
all the oceans . . . and the five continents, to cast them
down beyond Infinity at the foot of the throne of God.
That is Thy work . . .
And that is why, just now, dejected by our powerlessness,
inclining profoundly with Thy priest, like distressed men-
dicants,
we supplicate Thy Father to send us an angel
to carry to Thine altar on High
haec . . . haec omnia . . .
this huge mass . . . formidable for us,
For Thee, the Word, Who holdeth the world in the hollow of
Thy Hand, a mere straw!
We are waiting expectantly.

The Offertory of Jesus Christ . . .

Thou hearest us immediately, O Christ!
Thou answerest our supplications in person . . .
the Second Person, the Son of God . . .
Thou, the only Priest of heaven and earth . . .
for an angel would not do.
Only Thou art able to take this planet . . . Thine arms full
. . . Thy hands full . . .
the containing and the contained . . .
in sanctas ac venerabiles manus suas . . .
and to raise it as a Host even to the throne of the Father and to
give it back to Him . . . spiritualized . . . blessed . . .
sanctified . . . Yes! for that . . . there is none but Thee.
O admirable exchange!
Earth has given Thee its dust in order that Thou mightest
become man like us, and, in return, Thou hast given it Thy
Divinity.

134

This poor earth, heavily weighed down with sin,

Has been made light, has been steeped in the Blood which Thou
holdest out to Thy Father . . .

Thus dost Thou upset all the laws of weight and gravitation.
It no longer falls to earth, but to heaven.

It no longer seeks its foundations behind, but before . . . on
the Infinite heights where reigns Unalterable Majesty.

It is very clear, He wants *all: Omnis honor et gloria—*
the hazy radiance of human accomplishments which floats
like an aureole around monuments and museums and acad-
emies and libraries and military schools . . .

and especially the pure effulgence which rises from the fiery
footprints left on the ground by Thy saints,

all Beauty, all Holiness, all music, all glory, and all love . . .
Unwearyingly, Thou gatherest them together for Thy Father, O Christ,
as a painstaking gleaner who leaves not an ear behind,

and Thou puttest it back into His hands,

And we, tiny bits of creation . . . "negligible beginnings of
something which is not finished" . . .

we feel ourselves carried in this whirlwind with all the grains of
dust on earth, and restored to that ineffable place *in sinu
Patris*, that inexhaustible bosom of the Father of Lights,
whence we came out.

Such is that magnificent re-ascent which is accomplished in each
Mass . . . and which will be accomplishing itself even to
the end of time: *per omnia saecula saeculorum.*

Should we not be engulfed in adoration and put into our
Amen the utmost praise and acclamation of heaven and
earth?

XIV

AMEN

> The last word of the Canon . . .

It is the congregation which pronounces it . . .
> which is honored with having a say in this sacred moment . . .
> when, alone and in mystery, the celebrant speaks . . .
> rather, when Christ Himself speaks, through the mouth of His priest, in order to consecrate the Host.

It is the congregation which has the last word of the Canon! . . . and what a word!

> *Amen!* . . .

Of old, everyone present said it in a loud tone. Is it of this *Amen* that Saint Jerome speaks when he writes in his letters: "I still hear, in passing into the church, the thunder roll of the *Amen* which the people make in response to the celebrant"?

"The thunder," in any case, was not out of place, nor the lightning . . . nor the trumpets . . . nor the fanfares which sounded in accompaniment.

In all the liturgy of the Mass, after the words of Consecration . . . none are more weighty with meaning,
> none more sparkling with light and sound.

> *Per omnia saecula saeculorum. Amen.*

Forever and ever . . . Yes, Lord!
> Thou art the Master of the universe!
> To Thee alone, be all honor and glory in heaven and earth!
> *Amen!*

A word which should be reiterated and sung with a faith and love as great as the world, as deep as the past and the future—

"This word which circulates from star to star . . .
Everything on earth spells it; man alone articulates it."
(Lamartine)
"Little birds," said the Curé d'Ars, to the warblers in his
   garden, "you do not know what you are saying . . ."
There should be at least a few Christians here below who know
   what their singing means . . . What the warblers and the
   sparrows and the larks say in their chirpings should be ex-
   pressed in ritualistic and sacred syllables . . . *Amen!*
And not the birds only . . . but . . .

                                        all creation . . . all life.

The earth must breathe forth its soul!
   Benedicite omnia opera Domini Domino . . .
There must be a plebiscite of the stars and the oceans and the
   forests, and the harvests . . . to which all creatures at once
   may be invited to vote, to applaud unanimously the honor
   of their Lord.
Amen! Amen! O Lord God!
   Ye works of God, bless ye the Lord.
And likewise, all the life of the planet, all the essence of men
   and of things, of men and of the tools which are in their
   hands . . .
   all these explosions, this clamor, this uproar which rises
   from the streets, and the workshops, and the fields, and the
   oceans;
   the rumbling of motors and of machines.
The sighs of men working and their joyous whistling . . .
   this partridge call in the twilight,
   this mournful siren which sounds far over the sea and
   which sends a warning to harbors and to coasts:
all these beings which came from the bosom of God and which
   are seeking the way of return . . . must find their pass-
   word on the threshold of the Infinite . . .

And this word—rightfully—forms part of the grand Sacrifice of
praise which has been given to the entire world to express
worthily its prostrate Love.
Amen!
And it is I, insignificant baptised soul, who is commissioned to
utter it.
And it is I, who am the humble agent of heaven and earth.
This earth which has drunk the Blood of Christ can no longer
content itself with a mere man, to express its praise; it must
now have the Son of God.
And this Son of God is Christ, for me . . . for us . . . for all
of us in this church.
The stars, the birds, the forests, the seas and the fields . . .
offered by Christ to His Father,
await expectantly our consenting to this offertory in a
triumphant *Amen.*
Lord, let me not defraud them, nor let me defraud Thee, Thyself . . . betraying the Creator as well as the creatures.
Let me say this *Amen* with a full heart and into those two
resounding syllables, I place the whole universe
and all its Adoration, and all its faith, and all its Hope, and
its total abandonment to Love. *Per omnia saecula saeculorum* . . .
Amen!
But this word will be without import on my lips . . .
if it has not subdued my whole being,
if it does not express the entire offering of myself to God
all-powerful.

Amen! It is the "God only"

of the saints . . . so pure . . . so pure in their actions, their
occupations . . . preoccupations, that they would rather
be torn to pieces than attribute to themselves the slightest
glory.

Potius disrumpar . . . said Saint John Berchmans.

Yes! "Rather be broken in two . . ."

Amen! it is the "God only" of my perfection.

Nothing but God is of importance any longer in my life.

Here I completely lose myself in the magnificence of His glory and I renounce the management of this little universe which is stirring and quivering within me.

If I must capture in my *Amen*

all the Adoration of the whole world,

how can I honestly allow myself a spark of vanity?

Lord, in the *Amen* I now say,

I complete the task of giving Thee all,

and of casting myself, eyes closed, with all my soul and all my heart into this abyss of Thy holy Consecration . . .

Christ, I beseech Thee to take me in Thy holy Hands, where are already the five continents.

Take . . .

Only a few grains of dust . . . placed under Thy creating breath . . .

Finish, I beseech Thee, my creation by bearing me on to my Plenitude . . . even to my eternal Satiation . . .

into the arms of Thy Father, through the hands of Thee, His Son, in communion with the Holy Spirit . . .

per omnia saecula saeculorum . . . *Amen!*

FOURTH PART

The Participation in the Sacrifice Through Communion

From the Pater to the Communion

The Participation in the Sacrifice Through Communion

From the Pater to the Communion

To orientate the soul:

The grand Rule, the "Canon," of the participation of the faithful in the Sacrifice, is to offer the soul entirely to Christ Who is coming in all His Fullness.

Fundamental, indispensable preparation:

An Offertory in which you have offered your whole heart and all the course of your day . . . A Consecration in which you have cast, have sacrificed your whole life . . . The best preparation for Communion, as well for the ordained priest as for us, is the Mass.

With the *Pater*, begins the immediate preparation for the Communion:

"Give us this day our daily bread." This means particularly our spiritual bread.

"Forgive us our trespasses, as we forgive those who trespass against us." Christ will not have at the banquet brothers hostile to each other. They must be reconciled.

I

O Father, Give Us This Day Our Daily Bread

PATER NOSTER

Our Father Who art in Heaven . . .

If I address myself to Thee directly, I the least of Thy adopted
    children,
if I grant myself the infinite sweetness of calling Thee, "Father,"
    Thee, the immense, the inaccessible Majesty,
it is because the holy Liturgy of the Mass reminds me daily that
    I have been instructed, formed, by Thy Divine Son, and
    given an imperative mission:
    Sic ergo vos orabitis . . . you will say to "My Father."

Our Father . . .

For two thousand years, this Divine Formula has been used.
For ages, generations have recited their *Pater Noster.*
Even here, with this handful of Christians, the whole Church
    says the "Our Father" in union with the priest.
Together . . . this rich man, this laborer, this farm hand, this
    seamstress, this servant, this society lady . . . we all declare
    ourselves: Thy children; we proclaim ourselves to be in
    very deed brothers and sisters . . .
We acknowledge our sweet duty of loving Thee, of loving
    Thee with one and the same love,
and that . . . solemnly . . .

in the very heart of the Mass.

Hardly has Thy Son descended upon the altar, surrounded by
    His mystic guard, wholly devoted to Thy glory and Thy
    universal triumph,
hardly have we, all together, cast the whole course of our day
    into His Consecration, than He bids us recite His Prayer,

that we may be united with Him . . . the same fervor, the same brotherly love, the same universality of Love, the same entire and filial devotion.

"Our Father, Who art in Heaven, hallowed be Thy Name, Thy Kingdom come; Thy will be done on earth as it is in Heaven."

O majestic and divine Words! . . .

which come forth in all their vigor from the Heart of Thy Son:

His inmost Thought, His dearest Desire, expressed in human words . . .

the whole purpose of His thirty-three years of mortal life . . . and of His Presence here, now,

the whole reason also of our passage on earth.

No doubt, alone on the mountain at night, He said these words Himself . . . often.

And when He bids us: "Pray thus,"

it is His own Prayer that He gives us, a Prayer that He knows by heart. Therefore . . .

we dare . . .

Audemus dicere

We, poor sinners, we indeed, who retard, who thwart, who hinder Thy reign here below . . .

we dare, in spite of everything, to call Thee, "Our Father."

We dare, even, to make of Thee requests that sound more like commands:

"Hallowed be Thy Name" . . . "Thy Kingdom come."

Thou saidst to Saint Catherine of Genoa:

"It is not enough to ask; command!"

We are certain that according to the design of Thy Kingdom, no power, no hearing is denied us . . . and that we can come before Thee, with demands which are . . .

145

those of Thy Son, our Elder Brother, present amongst us, because it is
"through Him, with Him, in Him . . ."
that we live, speak, act henceforth . . .
because it is in Him that we render Thee, in union with the
Holy Spirit, all honor and glory:
to make souls docile to Thy Will, not only in the little corner
in which we live . . . but throughout the earth "as it is in
Heaven."
SUCH IS THE GREAT DREAM OF THE TRUE LAY-
MAN AND OF THE APOSTLE.
Prayer as wide as the universe, which overtakes every soul in its
distress . . . and every sinner in his sin . . .
Thou *must*, O Christ, be in us, that we may dare . . . we pyg-
mies . . . to say this Prayer of giants.

But, for that, we must live.

We must eat our daily bread!
O Father, it is Thy Will that we think of it . . .
And it is also Thy Will that we should eat to our fill, so that we
may recite sincerely our *Pater Noster* and live its first
four petitions.
And it is Thy Will that we ask to eat it every day, because
Thou art not only the Father Who gives life,
but the Father Who gives bread . . .
the Master of the harvest and the mills . . .
the First of husbandmen. Thy Divine Son has said:
Pater meus agricola est.
And so it is that Thou, O God, thinking of Thy children,
made fertile the great steppes and the plains, from Canada
even to the pampas of Argentina, not to mention the
Ukraine . . . that "granary of the world."

Alas! Thy children, little and great, forget it. To an ever greater extent, we find people who have never known it.

School books no longer teach it.

Since the beginning of the twentieth century, some even pretend that Thy wheat grows by itself and that the mills turn better without Thee.

Result: the barns are bursting, the granaries are cracking under the sacks . . . and the poorest of Thy children go without bread.

For them, for ourselves, O Father, we ask: give us this day our daily bread.

But especially, give us . . .

The supersubstantial Bread:

that which Thou didst first think of in creating the blade of wheat and the vast harvest, that which has just become the Flesh of Thy Son.

Give us every day this divine Bread . . . the nourishment of our souls which have grown languid, this Bread which is Thy Son Himself in us, that we may be strong in the daily struggle and immolate ourselves with Him.

This Bread of pardon and of love!

How can we, indeed, bear ill-will toward those who have trespassed against us and who come to Thy Table with us?

Christ has told us that we cannot come without being reconciled to one another . . . man to man, and also, strictly speaking, country to country, class to class . . .

O God Our Father, forgive us our trespasses as we forgive those who trespass against us.

Grant that we may be one in Thy Love and in Thy Heart, as all the grains of wheat in Thy Host are one.

O Our Father Who art in Heaven,

come down upon earth . . . Fill with Thy Spirit, our streets,

our shop windows, our places of work, where too often
alas! there is only sensuality and worldliness . . .

Lead not into temptation Thy poor sensuous children.

Deliver us from this frightful poison of hatred.

Increase throughout the world the number of those who sincerely recite their "Our Father," not through ostentation,
merely with their lips . . . but through the need of their
famished souls, for Thy Justice and Thy Love.

And grant that beyond the horizon where, alas, still rises the
smoke of our passions and our battles,

on a radiant slope, O Father of so many prodigal children,
Thou wilt appear, with Thine arms outstretched.

II

LORD, BE TO US A LAMB, AND NOT A JUDGE

"Lamb of God, Who taketh away the sins of the world . . .

As Thou comest nearer to us, grant that I may unite myself
more closely with Thy priest . . . and that I may with
greater depth of feeling, say with him:

'Have mercy on us! Have mercy on us!'
Thou knowest so well that we are wolves,
wolves . . . who do not even agree among themselves . . ."
Then . . . then . . .

grant us peace . . .

Clearly! our great unhappiness lies in our misunderstanding of
one another.

Since Thou hast been upon the altar, waiting for us, O Christ,
Thy sacred liturgy has multiplied its calls to peace, to
brotherly love.

Thou Who art gentleness itself . . . Thou Who hast the mildness of the lamb,

O Thou Who art the lamb of God who allowest Thyself
to be immolated without a cry,
grant us peace! Grant that we may love one another! . . .
Grant that we may rediscover the meaning of true brotherly love!
Grant that among families, that among competitors in sport
or business, we may be truly brothers.
And then begin . . .

the three prayers,

the only ones which prepare us immediately for Communion.
Lord, give us the grace to say them well, with Thy priest.
Let us taste their strength and fragrance!
Do not let us go seeking others . . . acts of surrender or of
desire . . . or of this . . . or of that . . . which are all
very good . . . but . . .
whether they be in music or in words,
anything which has the temerity to substitute itself for the
PRAYER, the only one which is fitting and complete,
the Prayer of Christ and His Church,
is insufficient . . . impertinent.

Lord Jesus Christ, Thou hast said:

"My peace I leave you, My peace I give unto you."
Lord Jesus, Who said that in the Cenacle, after having
celebrated the first Mass . . .
Lord Jesus, Who hast made of this word: PEACE, Thy Testament, Thy Last Word, Thy Commandment,
grant to the world that peace which the world cannot give.
Grant it at least to Thy children,
that they may be its living witnesses and apostles.
When, O Lord, will they come to an agreement . . .
family with family, nation with nation . . .
and also . . . diocese with diocese . . . parish with parish . . .

149

and Church with Church . . .

so that there will be . . . as we have just begged Thee . . .
but one fold under one shepherd, but one spirit, a conquering spirit, which nothing will resist because it will be
Thine . . .
Lord, when will that be? . . .

and that peace, dear Lord, begin by granting it to the poor
mendicant before Thee.

Regard not my sins.

Ne respicias peccata mea . . .

Do not regard me too closely! . . . look upon the good side
. . . not the bad!
not on that side which rightly goads Thy Justice, which
excites Thine Anger . . .

Do not look upon those leprous and crimson-colored stains:
my lies, the general lie of my life . . . my acts of cruelty
to Thy less fortunate ones . . . my immodesty, that forgetfulness of Thy Passion which is being continued . . .

Oh! my God . . . regard me on the good side.

. . . Look upon me in Thy Church.

Sed fidem ecclesiae tuae . . .

Regard me precisely . . .
there where Thou hast placed me . . . in the dazzling light
of Thy Saints.

Dear Lord . . . do not regard my laziness in rising in the morning . . . my indifference in participating in Thy Sacrifice
. . . in being Thy witness . . .

but look upon the magnificent eagerness with which Saint Andrew ran toward his cross.

Do not look upon *my* little sentimental weaknesses, my vain
susceptibilities, my silly cowardice when occasion arises to
defend Thee.

150

But on the contrary . . .

> look upon the passionate love of the heart of Saint Paul,
> the fearlessness of Saint Ignatius, of Saint Perpetua and of
> Saint Felicitas going to martyrdom.

Regard not *my* little selfish calculations . . .

> all my little tricks to bring notice to myself, to be the cen-
> ter of admiration of worldly galleries.

On the contrary, regard the conquering force of Thy great missionaries: Vincent Ferrer, Francis Xavier, Francis Regis . . .

> the untiring charity of Vincent de Paul . . . of the Curé
> of Ars and of Don Bosco.

Look upon the love of Thy Carmelites, of Thy two Theresas,
the great and the little . . . who are both great because
both made themselves little.

Please! regard not my sins . . .

> but the holiness of that Church, of Which I am, alas! the
> most wretched member . . . but all the same, a member.

Now, since they are of Thy Church and of Thy Body,

> O Christ, Thou wilt indeed
> in the Face of the inflexible Majesty of Thy Father,
> through a holy shame, cast over Thy pitiable and leprous
> members, if they repent, the sparkling mantle of Thy
> Beauty.

O Christ, be truly my Justice, my Wisdom, my Purity! Be my
Body, be my Spirit, be my Heart!

> Be my Lamb of God . . . and in the sweetness of Thy
> radiance, take away my sins, and those of the whole world.

And following Thy example, Lord, remembering Thine immense and princely charity toward me, I will never more
judge my brothers and my sisters outside the splendor of
Thy Mystical Body, snatching them arbitrarily apart from
it, and studying them to discover according to my own
judgment the shadows, the blemishes, and the wounds . . .

O Lamb of God, in the resplendence of Thy Sanctity, take

away the sins of my brothers and sisters; take away mine and those of the entire world.

O Lord Jesus Christ, Son of the Living God,

permit me to acknowledge Thee as our first Pope, Saint Peter, did, *Tu es Christus, Filius Dei vivi!*

May Thy Flesh and Blood which are going to penetrate within me, accomplish their work of union with the Father and the Holy Ghost.

Deliver me from my sins and negligence, from this deplorable laxity in prayer, because I rely only on myself, on my own strength.

Deliver me from this tendency to seek credit for myself, instead of showing Thee forth to souls.

I do not want to lose any part of the Priesthood that Thou givest to me . . .

I want to be entirely devoted to Thy interests . . .

And make me always adhere to Thy commandments *Et fac me tuis semper inhaerere mandatis . . .*

to Thy slightest wish, to all Thy commands.

The chief betrayal is mortal sin,

and also venial sin, when it is deliberate, which weakens us against mortal sin.

O Christ of my Mass, Who is coming to me,

O Thou Who art going to be so joined to my flesh and blood that we shall be but one, never permit me to be separated from Thee to the point of being at the left— Thou at the right. Thou in the church, in Thy tabernacle; and I at the factory, in the field, or at the bottom of the mine, or on my boat . . . without Thee.

Let there never be a time or place in which I shall detach my soul from Thy Soul, my spirit from Thy Spirit,

any more than I shall be able, in a few moments, to detach my flesh from Thy Flesh, and my blood from Thy Blood.

Let Thy Holy Spirit inspire me with a realization of the horror
of this separation . . . and let the very thought of that
abyss cast me into Thine Arms, O Christ, my Elder
Brother, and make me hunger and thirst for Thee.

And let this Communion which I am about to make

Non mihi proveniat in judicium . . .
not turn to my judgment before Thy tribunal.
Alas! I am so capable of bringing that upon myself.
I could so easily poison Thy pure and spotless Host,
    and make of the Lamb of God Who is coming to me,
    to love and to save me . . .
    a judge obliged to condemn me.
On the contrary, let this Host be my great safeguard!
    Let Its light, like a beacon in the night,
    point out the obstacles to me.
May it be my strength, my life, and my salvation!
May Thy Flesh nourish me daily,
    Thy Blood saturate me and teach me how I must suffer,
and with what nobility of soul one must live and die when he is
    Thy brother and Thy member.

O Christ, Thou Who livest and reignest . . .

being God with God the Father, in the unity of the Holy Ghost,
    forever and ever,
grant me the grace to hunger and thirst for Thy Love and Thy
    Life within me, and for Thy Passion,
so that, participating daily in Thy Sacrifice, every day I may
    save souls with Thee, being poor, humiliated, meek and
    humble of heart . . . like Thee.
O Lamb of God Who takest away the sins of the world!

THE CHRISTIAN-PRIEST

> "HE WHO EATS MY FLESH AND
> DRINKS MY BLOOD . . ."

It is the hour of Repast . . . O Father. Thou invitest us to eat
and to drink . . .
the Flesh and Blood of Thy Son.
He is there, on the altar . . . He is waiting . . . He is waiting
for Thy children, who have been invited to the Banquet,
and who have despoiled themselves of everything in order
to consume Him.
Despoilment of the Offertory . . .
for they have cast into it all they have and are!
Immolation of the Consecration . . .
for this brazier of the Sacrifice has consumed everything!
The Christian, consecrated, immolated, awaits his Christ,
and his Christ awaits him.
Lord, I am not worthy . . . but say only the word . . .
the word of absolution . . .
If we have lost grace, it must be sought, not from Christ
of the altar . . . but of the same Christ, nevertheless, Who
is under another species . . . in the confessional.
Words of encouragement, of purification, of preparation: the
whole Mass is there, from the Psalm *Judica me . . .* to
the three prayers which follow the *Agnus Dei*,
to prepare, to make beautiful again this first sacerdotal ornament
of my soul: the invisible alb of grace required for the
Sacrifice
which culminates in the Banquet.
But the great Word which sustains and makes me less unworthy
of receiving Thee,
Thou hast said, O Christ, at the Consecration:

"This is My Body . . . This is My Blood . . ."
Who can tell the beauty of a soul offered with the Host!
My Communion will not have its full value . . . its real splen-
	dor . . . and its plenitude of meaning and strength . . .
unless it is:

a sacerdotal Communion,

that is to say, a Communion in union with the Communion of
	the priest, who is celebrating in the name of all . . .
a Communion of the baptised layman who has just offered, to-
	gether with the priest, and through his hands, the Host,
a Communion which *forms part of the Mass* . . . which is the
	participation and the completion of the Sacrifice . . . and
	not only . . .

the simple visit of a friend . . .

Indeed, O Jesus, Thou art my Friend, and I am Thine,
	as Thou didst so delicately tell Thine Apostles.
But, in spite of my wretchedness, permit me to lift my hopes
	high . . .
	In Thy Sacrifice I would be . . . more than a friend, well
	served . . . aided . . . comforted. I would be content
	only if my friendship tended, at least, to become like
	Thine, a great Love . . . which gives all for all.
And that is why, O sublime Operator of our Salvation, I want
	to be with Thee . . . fully sacrificed, at the time when
	Thou dost give the utmost . . .
	at the time when Thou givest all, when Thou comest to
	us with all Thy Heart, with all Thy Blood, with all Thy
	Life . . .
I wish to communicate during Mass . . . at the most intense
	moment of Labor . . . and of Love.

Too often, alas! . . . it is indeed necessary! . . . for reasons
of work or of health . . .

I communicate before or after Mass.

Better to communicate thus than not at all . . .
but let it be done reluctantly!
And even then I struggle to attach these Communions, made in
haste and apart from the Mass, to the Holy Sacrifice which
never ceases throughout the world.
Let me try to graft an immense and generous love on what
threatens to become mere routine.
For, in forming this habit, I risk making little of my Christ . . .
of going to His Banquet only for the dessert . . .
To communicate thus is to eat outside of the repast . . . it is to
eat quickly . . . too quickly,
"it is not good for the health."
And besides, it is to go to Communion seeking gain for *oneself*,
when Christ is expecting to communicate with one who is
seeking strength to assist in the great battle for souls.
For the devout soul, there is only Christ . . .
Christ in Sacrifice,

Christ of Golgotha.

Risen! Without question . . . Glorious, radiant! Yes!
But Christ Who has suffered, and Whose sufferings, though
past, are being continued, now . . . at this very moment,
to save the world, and Who is asking me for "a helping
hand" to "fill up what is wanting in His Passion."
Lord, I know! . . . Thou hast already told me and Thou tellest
me again:
"I can suffer no more. But lend me your own sufferings
and I will give them my strength. We two! I am relying
on your sacrifice, to lead such or such a soul to absolution
and to my Banquet."

156

O Christ, I understand! Thou wouldst set Thy Mass, Thy Sacrifice, forever in my soul.

Although I am only baptised and confirmed, Thou desirest that I, a simple layman, should make the communion of a priest . . . and even

the Communion of a saviour of the world!

Surely this is too lofty an ambition, dear Lord!

But no . . . for in the seclusion of our chapel, or in the great silent naves of the cathedrals, bowed down in prayer,

when I am straining every effort to be recollected . . . to concentrate all my thoughts on Thee:

Lo, Thou comest to me . . . and I meet in Thee all my brethren . . .

A figure of speech, of course! They are not *corporally* in Thee . . .

but Thou, Thou Whom I receive, *Thou art* in them . . .

Thou art their Head, their Vine . . . their Center . . . their Heart . . . their Life . . .

Thy Heart is the immense sanctuary whence are breathed forth all the wailings of their anguish . . . and the burning desires of their love.

And it is all-reechoing and throbbing with these outcries that Thou descendest into me.

O Christ, Thou hast but one mind,

one Heart . . . one Prayer and one Life with all.

Impress upon my mind that in China, in Japan, at the front with our armies, and in the rear likewise, in my place of work . . . in my home . . .

there is need of my Offertory, of my Host, of my Mass! . . .

There is need of a Communion which is the Mass prolonged.

O Christ universal and Catholic, permit me to enter with Thee into the hearts of my brethren . . . and let me devote myself to their welfare.

Thou hast struck down all partitions, all barriers, all frontiers, in order to show Your love for us.

Perform the same work in me . . . and because Thou art in me, let nothing remain to separate me from Thee!

And let me realize that to live in Thee is to live a life open to everyone . . . like Thine Arms; given to everyone . . . like Thy Bread . . .

it is to live with such a complete gift of self that I would die for those whom Thou hast entrusted to me . . .

Lord, whither art Thou leading me?

To what limits? . . . I am afraid.

But no! Fear nothing! I have changed the face of the earth. I just this moment changed bread and wine into My Body and My Blood . . . *Si vis* . . . If you will it . . . It is no trouble for me to change you into Myself.

The Thanksgiving of Christ and of the Whole Church Within Us

From the "Quod Ore Sumpsimus" to the Prayers after Mass

The Thanksgiving of Christ and of the Whole Church Within Us

From the "Quod Ore Sumpsimus" to the Prayers after Mass

To orientate the soul:

Christ has returned to us, after having surrendered into the bosom of the Father, *in sinu Patris*, all that we cast into His Consecration: our tiniest actions, our slightest movements, all the activity throughout the course of the day. He restores it to us a hundredfold, and it is in HIM that we have our Life and the sanctification of the hours we are going to live. Left to ourselves, we should be powerless to give thanks for such a marvelous grace.

But, nourished by the same Divine Flesh, Christians . . . priests and faithful . . . form one single Bread, one single Body, one and the same sacerdotal family. Together, then, united with their Head, Christ, let them give thanks! It will be Christ Himself Who will, for them, give thanks to the Infinite Majesty. And united in thanksgiving and in prayer, let us never desist from loving one another.

161

During the last minutes . . . the last great movements of the
    Mass,
    why leave the priest?
Let us follow him to the end.

                            Thanksgiving . . . together!

It is that of the Church . . . consequently, ours!
    that which is made daily by the priests
    beginning with the Pope and the Bishops
    at their Mass . . . which is ours.
Do you think of that? . . . Every day, saying
    the same prayer as the Pope! . . .
With him, with all priests, let us ask that "what we have taken
    with our mouths, we may receive with a pure heart," the
    gift of the all-loving Father: His Son Jesus, Who has re-
    turned to us from Heaven,
        with all that He lovingly and eternally offers us: His Holi-
        ness, His Purity, His Truth, His Love . . . *omni bene-*
        dictione coelesti et gratia . . .
so many remedies against our castles in the air, our vain conceit,
not harshly imposed on our wandering thoughts . . .
    gently . . .

                            Let us rest on Christ.

Let us, with the priest, humbly ask Him:
    "May Thy Body, O Lord, which I have received and Thy
    Blood which I have drunk, cleave to my inmost heart,"
    not just at the surface, but into the innermost fibers of my
    being.
And where Infinite Purity passes through,
    may there remain no old stains . . .
    of concupiscence . . .
    of foolish conceit . . .

It is the divine moment in which we are heard . . .
Grace is present . . . The Fountain is present! . . .
Let us drink! . . . Let us drink to the full!
At the Offertory we have asked that
"we may become partakers of His Divinity, Who has con-
descended to become partaker of our humanity."
And now His Divinity penetrates us from head to foot . . .
The day which we are about to live is His as well as ours.
We could make no more appropriate Thanksgiving,
no more efficacious prayer: the continuation of the Mass.
It is the Way of the Cross continuing in Thanksgiving: a
Thanksgiving which is made in Sacrifice.
Let us not fail, then, to read with the priest
The Communion and the Postcommunion . . .
after which, "Go, you are dismissed."
Not, however, until we have received . . .

the unparalleled Blessing.

After the *Ite, Missa est*, the *Placeat tibi Sancta Trinitas,*
prayer after the Mass, formerly separate from it . . .
the priest up to the end asks that his Sacrifice may be acceptable
and may obtain forgiveness for himself . . .
and for all those for whom he has offered it.
Then he kisses the altar and makes over the congregation a
great Sign of the Cross:
a blessing which is a prayer at the same time that it is a purification and a light which descend from the Father, the Son,
and the Holy Spirit,
likewise a sacramental which gets its nourishment at the
Highest Source.
It is in the name of the Lord Jesus that the priest calls down
upon us . . .
the blessing of blessings, a visible sign of interior graces

which have been granted, a synthesis as well as a symbol
of all the benefits of the Mass.

Is not the Mass an unparalleled Blessing?

Initium sancti evangelii secundum Joannem . . .

the beginning of the Gospel according to Saint John . . .
"And the Word was made Flesh and dwelt among us."

Formerly, the priest said these words immediately after the
Communion.

And these words are so characteristic of the Mass!

Is not the Word again made Flesh . . . upon the altar?

Does It not dwell among us?

Gospel of Saint John . . . Gospel of Christmas . . . Gospel of
every Mass . . .

precious Gospel which the early Christians venerated, carrying
it in a little bag around the neck . . . having it placed
with them in the tomb . . .

It was the lively expression of their faith, even as it was the
means of their preservation . . .

Our ancestors in the Faith loved it and our great-grandmothers
used to recite it by the light of a candle, in the midst of
storms.

Are there no longer storms in the times in which we live?

Yes . . . but our great-grandmothers are no more, and this
candle . . . ingenuous and artless witness of the light . . .
was extinguished with them in their burial . . .

In the main . . . these stalwart old Christians . . .
whether they wished it or not . . .

were witnesses of the Light

Of Him Who is its eternal Provision,

of Him Who gives of it to every man who appears in this world
. . . his share . . . just enough to give him an insatiable
thirst for the Source.

164

Saint John is a witness that on Thabor, at the Resurrection, at
the Ascension, he was royally served.

Full Spring of all Truth, of all Beauty, of all Life . . . which
is perpetually gushing up in us, and which in its all-pure
engendering, free from all sensual caprice, makes us, indef-
initely, children of God . . .

make us happy with Thy plenitude.

Make us the radiant bearers of Jesus Christ.

O my brothers and sisters who have just communicated and
who bear Christ home with you,

Please! Let the Gospel of Saint John
keep you company!

Radiant Gospel . . . worthy of Jesus Christ!

Gradually, the people became so importunate
that they obtained the favor of the priest's reciting it after
the blessing.

As they were coming out of the church, they desired that this
flame would go with them into the street.

It was like the lamp of the Lamb and of the Spouse.

And these living tabernacles of the Christ of the Mass went to
their homes . . . to their work . . .
accompanied by this Light.

Thus, the candles went before the Host,

and it was no longer true that "his own received Him not."

To Live One's Mass

To Live One's Mass

I

Go! The Mass is over. Yes!

But it is never ended . . . it goes on.

It goes on in the church during the ten minutes of our private thanksgiving . . . or rather, of the thanksgiving of Christ within us . . .

for, let us allow Him to pray, sing, adore . . . in union with all our brothers and sisters in Him.

It goes on in Heaven: Christ stands perpetually before His Father, a brilliant Victim offering Himself with mankind which He never ceases to redeem.

It goes on, on earth . . . at two o'clock in the afternoon, at six o'clock in the evening, in such and such a corner of the world it is six, seven, eight o'clock in the morning, and at this very moment, priests are saying: *Introibo ad altare Dei . . . Suscipe sancta Pater, omnipotens aeterne Deus . . . Hoc est enim corpus meum.*

The Mass is never ended.

As long as there are on the earth

poor little ones who are hungry . . .

orphans who have never known the Father . . .

prodigals far from their Father's house, who feed themselves on husks . . .

169

the Mass goes on.

But what affects me most deeply is that

my Mass never ends,

this Mass which is very particularly mine, in which I have intimately participated and communicated, this morning.

This Mass will go on and on till the next Mass . . . that of tomorrow, or the day after, or of next Sunday.

I have just cast into my Offertory and into the Consecration
all my activities.

Christ has taken all that I had gathered, to bathe my offering in the very Glory of God . . .

Then . . .

He has returned to me resplendent, and now dwells in His
temple within me.

I bear Him! . . .

as a living and invisible Ostensorium, through the streets.

I carry Him into the bus, into the subway, the train, into
my house, my office, my factory, wherever my work calls
me.

It is no longer I who live; it is He.

It is He and I who write this letter, who sharpen this
pencil . . .

who calculate this wholesale price . . .

who pedal this sewing machine, or bicycle . . .

insignificant deeds . . . acts without import . . . ordinary
words . . . so many unexpected rites accessory to the Sacrifice into which I plunged myself this morning, surrender-
ing therein my whole life.

My Mass goes on.

So, Christ at Nazareth, taking up His tools or His water jug
. . . going to the synagogue or to the house of a customer
to carry to him his chair or his bench which had been
mended . . .

170

O little Christ, thus Thou didst begin Thy Mass. Thy least acts, Thy tiniest movements were redeeming deeds, accidental rites of the great Sacrifice which, at the age of thirty-three, Thou wouldst offer on Golgotha.

Thus . . . I fill up in the same way, what Thou didst begin . . . Thy Sacrifice.

The duties of my state of life become adoration.

In this page that I am writing . . . in the piece of work I am supervising . . . in this scissors with which I am cutting . . . I see Thine Adorable Will, and Thy Son, in me, adores It.

He devoutly wishes it to be fulfilled . . . and so do I . . . I would rather be torn to pieces than not do it.

In effect, what can hinder my adoring . . . with a brush in my hand, or a shovel, or a pickax, or a pair of scissors, or a fountain pen, or a broom, or a fork? . . .

My slight action this morning, which took such a short time, moulded into the Adoration of the Son of God, is thus extended to Infinity . . . It is inscribed on the altar on high . . . in the presence of His August Majesty.

Without need of a direct intention and a precise act, by all my daily work

and by my attitude,

if I have not broken the contact by serious sin, I adore the thrice holy God, as did Joseph, the carpenter, and his Apprentice, Jesus . . . while working . . .

I adore and I expiate.

My expiation,

my work becomes redemptory.

By my work, I expiate my faults. I expiate those of souls whom God has entrusted to me, those of the people who throng around them.

This morning, I delivered myself, body and soul, to my Christ.

I said to Him: "Take! Receive!"

It was my host in His.

It was my labor and my sweat and the blood of my veins lending to the mystic symbol the sharp reality of human blood, adding to the inexhaustible and bloody capital of Golgotha my poor little actual sufferings.

While writing, while sweeping, talking on business matters, using a typewriter, handling pick or shovel . . . doing simply what I ought to be doing during these twenty-four hours I am saving souls . . . I am helping the Blood of Christ to give life to such and such a dying member.

It is, on the spiritual plane, like a transfusion of blood.

My Mass continues, and I am carried along with all my actions of every minute, in the unfolding of Its fruitful course.

At each instant, I feel pressed to give all to my Christ Who is calling me and all the souls depending on my devotion.

O Lord, may I be indeed Thy perpetual host . . . may my whole life be my sacrifice, and especially may my death be my last Mass.

In that last moment, like so many saintly priests, may I say, *Introibo ad altare Dei.*

May my whole life be . . .

my thanksgiving and my prayer.

As long as My Mass continues, in all my actions, Lord, Thou wilt be uninterruptedly giving thanks to Thy Father.

Thou desirest that I be at my work, and on the other hand, that always and everywhere, I render thanks to God: *Semper et ubique gratias agere,* and that my prayer should rise unceasingly, *orate sine intermissione.*

How can I do this really and fittingly if Thou Thyself dost not assure this service in me?

If my activity of every minute has been cast this morning into Thy Consecration, hast Thou not already transformed my work into Thy Prayer?

If the stars and the flowers and the great planets give praise, is it
  forbidden me to hope that my fountain pen, or my broom,
  or my needle . . . or my machine, or my boat . . . or
  what-not . . .
should become, thanks to Thee and to me, tools . . .
  a factory of thanksgiving and of prayer.
I left the church this morning, bearing my Christ, that is to say:
  The Living Prayer, the Prayer fervent and always burning
  . . . the Prayer Triumphant.
As long as I have not denied Thee, O my Christ,
as long as I remain pliable in Thy Hand,
  Thou askest nothing better than to use me. Thou art jealous
  of letting nothing in my soul escape: and of its little acts,
  Thou makest a hymn of glory.
And of my sins?
In my poor soul, soiled and entangled,
  it is even my weakness and failures Thou turnest, because
  of the repentance and more humble love which follows . . .
into a kind of praise! . . .
into a veritable enriching . . .
into pieces of gold which have been lost and which Thou hast
  found again so joyfully.
O Thou, Creator of gold and of diamonds, delicate Goldsmith,
  make out of the dust and dross of my wretchedness
  the jewels which Thou desirest and of which Thy Evan-
  gelists speak.
I am ready to sell all, to lose all,
  to buy this pearl: *LOVE.*

                                        Thus my daily task

is my Mass.
That is to say, a burning holocaust
  not from the fire of my love, but from the fire of Thine.
  I do not even feel it.

Perhaps I do not even think of it; that is all too evident!
But, wherever life calls me,
it is Thou, my Christ, Who lovest in me.
　　It is Thou Who singest; it is Thou Who adorest;
　　It is Thou Who savest souls,
　　for of myself, what can I do?
Thou wishest, O God, Our Father, not to lose a single soul nor
　　anything of heaven and earth, and at every instant, Thy
　　priests must offer Thee this tribute of homage and of adora-
　　tion which Thy Jealousy exacts.
On the other hand, priests cannot come in alb and chasuble
　　. . . nor even in soutane, into our workshops and our fac-
　　tories.
It is then I, your priest by Baptism and Confirmation,
　　without other embellishment than my working clothes,
　　who must offer to God, through the Christ of my Mass, all
　　the work, all that activity, all that human labor which must
　　not be lost in myself or in others.
Christ in me will transform it into adoration and into love.

Resolution

How I must respect my dignity!
　　What probity in my stewardship!
　　What loyalty in my Service!
　　Through Christ and in Christ, at every hour of the day and
　　of the night, I am in the service of God and of the Church:
to be a Christ-merchant, a Christ-manufacturer, a Christ-lawyer
　　or banker,
　　a Christ-artisan or simple laborer,
　　to serve God our Father,
　　to serve my brothers and my sisters in Him,
　　and not to serve myself.
What is this new economy in which even in business "the last
　　shall be first"?

174

I shall need my Mass of tomorrow and the next day, and all those of this year, to learn that "the increase" will not be given me unless I seek first

the Kingdom of Heaven.

The Mass in 500 Years...
1,000 or 2,000 Years

The Last Mass

As long as there is an earth and men who are being born and
    who are dying,
    Thine altar, O Jesus, will remain in the world, visible, ac-
    cessible to the least among us of no matter what generation.
Is it not for that, and to honor Thy Father, that Thou, the
    Creating Word, launched our planet through space?
    like an immense train . . .
    a train that would turn around a mountain . . .
    even

                the holy Mountain . . .

which is spoken of in Psalm 42 *in montem sanctum tuum et in
    tabernacula tua.*
    At each instant . . . and everywhere we see an altar pre-
    pared, and the lights of a sacrifice that is being accom-
    plished!
See below there . . . a priest going up to the altar.
Ten minutes pass . . . and the train rolls at high speed . . .
    and yet . . . there on the right . . . do you see?
    The Mountain has not budged. The Cross is above and the
    Host is raised . . .
    It is the Elevation . . .

176

Ten minutes pass . . . and the train rolls at high speed . . .
　　and yet . . . there again it is the same . . .
Ten hours . . . ten years . . . ten centuries pass.
　　Other travelers are in the train . . . but . . .
　　the Mountain is always there.
　　And the Sacrifice is going on.
　　And the whole world is called to participate in it.
　　Do you hear? . . . Do you hear the bell which sounds . . .
　　for the *Introibo ad altare Dei?*

　　　　　　　　　　　And in 2,000 years, in 10,000 years,

as long as Thou hast not stopped the train, O Christ, it will be
　　the same.
　　The Cross is the axis of the world.
　　The planet is the Repository of the Host.

　　　　　　　　　　　　　　In a perpetual present,

O Christ, through space and time,
　　Thou seekest Thy members,
　　Thou pursuest with Thine immolation and Thy Blood, all
　　those of the twentieth, of the twenty-second, of the
　　twenty-third century . . . and so on.
And Thou askest of the universe, each day increased, as if it
　　were one single living soul,
　　the *Amen* of Adoration and of Love.
Then . . . how . . .
　in the simple passing of the twenty-four hours of my day . . .
am I of such a short memory and of such foolish lightheaded-
　　ness, to let fade out
　　my morning Sacrifice?
Grant, O dearly beloved Lord, that never will Thy Cross dis-
　　appear entirely from before my eyes!
　　Give me rather that grace that will keep it always before
　　me.

Did not Thy saints firmly fix their gaze on Thy Blood-
soaked Body?
Did they not drink from Thy Wounds, Thy Love, and
their sanctity?
How can I not be captured by this thought . . . that . . .
Thou art indeed more Christ of the present
than Christ of the past? . . .
Dost Thou even have a past?
As Man, Thou hast only a "yesterday."
And Saint Paul warns us of it.
Yesterday . . . arbitrary cutting of time . . .
a leaf fallen from the calendar of men,
or the simple ticking of their watches!
For Thee, yesterday is only today reinforced.
Jesus Christus heri et hodie, Ipse in saecula. (Hebr. XIII, 8)
There is only one Christ, the same whatever may be the hour,
the day, the year, the century or the centuries.
Yesterday, was the Cenacle . . . Yesterday . . . Golgotha.
But it was for today.

In a permanent today,

in an eternal present
Thou hast loved me always, as Thou lovest me now.
Thou hast contained me always,
Thou hast lived in me always,
as Thou containest me, as Thou livest in me now . . .
Ipse in saecula . . .
and thus for ages . . .
Yesterday . . . on the 14th day of the month of Nisan . . .
at the ninth hour . . . we say, at three o'clock in the afternoon . . .
Thou sawest me just as I am now,
occupied in writing . . . or in weeding my garden . . .
or in sewing . . . in laboring . . . in suffering perhaps.

Thou didst love with an ineffable love in my labor.
Thou didst consecrate to me Thy last sigh . . . Thy last
drop of Blood . . . in one great cry.

O Christ, so distant and so near,

O Christ, Who never ceasest to die . . .
because Thou art the eternal living One,
There is not a minute of time to come
Which Thou hast not lived intensely.
All the centuries rush in great waves to beat against Thy Holy
Mountain and receive their share of the Divine, before re-
bounding with Thee, through Thee, in Thee, even to the
throne of God.
In Ipso . . . omnis honor et gloria . . .
Thus goes the world . . . thus turns around the Host the
dazzling train of the stars and of the ages.
So, even to the last day . . . even to the last gathering to-
gether of peoples and of continents . . .

for the last Mass here below.

And as Thou didst say the first . . . and all the others, it is
Thou, the one Priest, Who wilt say the last.
May that last judgment, when the figure of this world will pass
away,
be a triumphant High Mass
served by the whole world!
Let us all conspire with Thee each day,
for that last day,
that all our Masses may be for the last!
May we each day, when delivering ourselves up in Thy Consecration, give Thee our life, that there may be an ever
greater number in the Church Militant who will aid the
great work of saving souls.

If our fervor, alas! cannot reduce to zero
    the number of the damned,
    let it at least each day increase
    the number of the blessed!
Lord, with Saint Theresa of the Child Jesus, we beg that on that
    day Thy Family will be complete.
    It is the last of all Masses.
    There is no question of coming
    after the Gospel . . . and then . . .
                Let the last deceits and the last phantoms
Vanish with the last smoke.
All the tombstones are overturned
There are no more cemeteries . . . There are no more
    churches . . .
    There are no more tabernacles . . .
    There are no more wheatfields, no more vineyards . . .
Finished the Kingdom of appearances! . . .
    appearances of bread and of wine . . .
    for there is no longer need of Consecrations,
    nor of Repositories, nor of Hosts!
Alone, there remains in Heaven, on the great high altar, before
    the Divine Majesty, in *sublime altare*, in *conspectu divinae*
    Majestatis . . .
                the eternal and heavenly Oblation
of the Son of Man, Whose full grown Body
    has attained Its Majority
    per omnia saecula saeculorum.

                                     AMEN.

A NOTE ON THE TYPE
IN WHICH THIS BOOK IS SET

This book is set in Janson, a Linotype face, created from the early punches of Anton Janson who settled in Leipzig around 1670. This type is not an historic revival, but rather is a letter of fine ancestry, remodelled and brought up to date to satisfy present day taste. It carries a feeling of being quite compact and sturdy. It has good color and displays a pleasing proportion of ascenders and descenders as compared to the height of the lower case letters. The book was composed and printed by The York Composition Company of York, Pa., and bound by Moore and Company of Baltimore. The typography and design by Howard N. King.